- 6 APR 2013

BIG BOOK OF
BBQ

BIG BOOK OF
BBQ

Delicious and inspiring recipes for
barbecues, griddle pans and hot plates

First published in 2010 by
New Holland Publishers (UK) Ltd
London • Cape Town • Sydney • Auckland

Garfield House
86–88 Edgware Road
London W2 2EA
www.newhollandpublishers.com

80 McKenzie Street
Cape Town 8001
South Africa

Unit 1, 66 Gibbes Street
Chatswood
NSW 2067
Australia

218 Lake Road
Northcote
Auckland
New Zealand

10 9 8 7 6 5 4 3 2 1

ISBN 978 1 84773 552 2

Editor: Amy Corstorphine
Design: Peter Gwyer
Production: Laurence Poos
Editorial Direction: Rosemary Wilkinson

Reproduction by Pica Digital Pte Ltd, Singapore
Printed and bound in Malaysia by Times Offset (M) Sdn Bhd

Contents

Introduction

This is a book about grilling, not just about barbecue.

In the American South, barbecue is a noun not a verb. By American definition, barbecue is a tough cut of meat cooked slowly over a wood-fired grill. The meat is basted with a simple vinegar - or sometimes tomato-based sauce. The result is meltingly tender, smoke-infused meat. But, if I can generalize, where there's smoke, there's fire. And where there's fire, there are men. And where there are men, there's competition. In America, whole states, cities, neighbourhoods and families are divided by barbecue. Take North Carolina, for example. Texas generally unites behind beef brisket, South Carolina is devoted to its mustard-based pork, while Kansas City loves its ribs. In North Carolina, however, things aren't so simple. On the western side of the state (Lexington or Piedmont), barbecue means a hog shoulder basted with a red, tomato-based sauce. Over in the east, on the other hand, they follow the old, North Carolina adage – use every part of the pig except for the squeal – with a little vinegar-based sauce to help it along. Both claim to have the best barbecue, and neither will budge. This debate isn't new; it is a controversy that has been simmering away for years, but recently there was a major development. In the spring of 2005 a city by-law was passed naming Lexington, with its pork shoulder and tomato-based sauce, the "Barbecue Capital of the World". Vinegar purists were up in arms. Friendships died, fists were drawn and reporters gathered. I caught the breaking news in my kitchen in Halifax, Nova Scotia as I innocently prepared a marinade for my pork ribs. I was listening to a North America-wide live radio programme, and I could feel the heat right through the radio.

At least the people of North Carolina agree on one thing – the use of the word "barbecue". Roger Dennis, a North Carolina newspaper columnist and barbecue devotee, set his readers straight when he wrote the following: "Barbecue – for the thousandth time – is a noun. It is not a verb or an adjective. You cook a pig and you get barbecue. You grill steaks and burgers. You do not "barbecue" anything. So shut up about it".

We're passionate about cooking anything alfresco. We love the way aromas waft through the garden, calling guests to gather by the flame. We crave the effects of a smoky charcoal, especially when accompanied by a handful of aromatic wood chips. We appreciate the ease and immediacy of a gas grill, and value the versatility of the griddle pan. They all capture the essence of casual dining, regardless of the weather, the season, or the time of the day. We're girls who are devoted to the grill. With this devotion comes strength and wisdom. We are strong enough to grill with the guys, but wise enough to avoid the competition that shrouds all things "barbecue".

We're not certain why competition follows flame. Maybe it's the primal action of meat to fire. Perhaps it's the over-sized tools. Regardless of reason, grilling not only tears up towns, it divides friends. When people get together for

barbecues in New Zealand, the guys elbow their way to the barbecue with beer and raw steaks in hand, while the women casually toss salads and sip wine in the kitchen. Thousands of kilometres away in Halifax, Nova Scotia, you'll find exactly the same scenario in their back gardens. But history, as they say, is meant to be broken. Women can grill, men can make salads, and anyone can turn a noun into a verb.

The word barbecue is much older than the dish. The Tainos (a Haitian tribe obliterated by European explorers) used the word *barbacoa* to describe a framework of sticks used for sleeping on or cooking over. The word was borrowed by the Spanish, and worked its way into the English language as barbecue at the end of the seventeenth century, still referring to a wooden framework. By the early eighteenth century, barbecue was exclusively a device upon which to roast meat; by the end of that century, its meaning was extended to any dish that was cooked upon such a device.

Many say the word derives from the French barbe à queue, literally "beard to tail", referring to the practice of spit-roasting whole animals.

Regardless of provenance, however, it's safe to say that the word "barbecue" has had a chequered semantic history. But we're laid back folks – we don't care whether we grill, barbecue, or barbecue "barbecue". What we do care about is taste. Flavour. Fresh ingredients. Global influences. Straightforward methods. Casual gatherings. Friends. Family. And, most of all, the relaxed feeling that only comes from cooking food over fire.

Successful barbecuing

Barbecuing can be a breeze if you follow our simple guidelines. Successful barbecuing calls for thought and planning: remember to think like a scout and BE PREPARED. How often have you sunk your teeth into a suspiciously pink chicken leg or been served a slightly over-charred sausage? These all too common occurrences can be easily avoided if you follow our easy instructions. Our marinating and food safety tips apply as much to indoor grilling as they do to outdoor cooking.

Marinating tips

■ For mess-free marinating and an even, all-over coating, place your ingredients in a strong plastic bag. If you have no large plastic bags or are marinating meat on skewers then always use non-corrosive dishes such as Pyrex, glass or stainless steel and cover tightly with clingfilm to avoid other foods tainting the flavour.

■ If you are marinating your meat for longer then 30 minutes always do so in the fridge. Remove it only 30 minutes before cooking to bring it back to room temperature.

■ In some recipes we heat the marinade. This speeds up the marinating time. Do not, however, heat marinades containing milk products such as yogurt and do not use hot marinades on fish, because they will begin to cook it immediately on contact. Hot, not boiling, marinades should be poured over the meat and left for no longer than 30 minutes at room temperature just prior to cooking.

■ Never mix raw foods such as fish and chicken in the same marinade – for maximum safety, keep foods separate.

■ Never combine cooked meat with your uncooked marinade. Instead, use the uncooked marinade during cooking for basting the meat.

■ If your marinade has a high sugar content it will burn more easily. Always hold off basting with these marinades until at least halfway through cooking. Always ensure that the last basting has had sufficient cooking. A low-sugar content marinade can be used to baste the meat from the start of cooking.

■ Before placing marinated items on the barbecue shake off any excess marinade, particularly if there is oil in it, to prevent flaring and burning.

■ Never use your best extra virgin olive oil in a marinade. It will burn and smoke because of the high content of monounsaturated fatty acids. Use light olive oil or vegetable oil instead, and save your best oil for salad dressings.

■ Acids are an important ingredient in marinades as they help break down enzymes and tenderize the meat. Common acid ingredients found in marinades are lemon juice, yogurt, wine, soy sauce and vinegar. Some fruits such as kiwi fruit and pomegranate are also highly acidic and are common meat tenderizers.

■ Do not over-marinate your meat. You may gain in flavour by doing this but you will also lose in texture. Some acidic marinades will break down the meat or fish if left too long.

Food safety and hygiene
Food safety is an important issue when it comes to barbecuing, keeping in mind that it is usually a hot summer's day when the barbecue comes out. When you're barbecuing, the greatest risk of food poisoning comes from raw and undercooked meats. Bugs such as E.coli, salmonella and campylobacter can cause serious illness. Follow these simple steps to avoid illness:

■ Always wash your hands thoroughly before and after handling raw meats.

■ Always keep your food cool, covered and out of the reach of animals and children.

■ All meats should be thoroughly defrosted before cooking. The best way to do this is to defrost them in the fridge overnight.

■ All marinated foods should be refrigerated until about 30 minutes before cooking unless a hot marinade has been used (see page 10). Take chicken out no longer than 30 minutes before cooking.

■ Use separate dishes to transfer uncooked and cooked meats and never combine the two.

■ Check your meat is at a safe temperature for eating; insert a meat thermometer into the thickest part of the flesh so it is as close as possible to the centre of the meat. Avoid contact with bones, which will give you an inaccurate reading. The temperatures should read approximately:

Beef/lamb/venison = 60–65°C (140–149°F) for medium-rare, 70–75°C (158–167°F) for well done. The meat should feel soft but firm and should still be juicy.

Pork = 65–70°C (149–158°F). The meat should be opaque throughout but still juicy.

Chicken = the flesh should be opaque throughout with no traces of pink and the juices should run clear when a skewer is inserted into the thickest part of the flesh.

■ Don't assume that meat charred on the outside will be cooked properly on the inside. Check that the centre of the food is piping hot, particularly when cooking chicken, burgers, sausages and kebabs.

■ Always have a bucket of sand nearby just in case the flames get out of hand.

TOOLS OF THE TRADE

Long tongs
These are essential for turning meats. Avoid any with sharp teeth or you will pierce the meat, and juices will be lost causing flare-ups and tough, dry results.

Wide spatula
A useful tool when dealing with whole chickens, pizzas or any large items. Ideally a pizza paddle with a long handle will do the job best. Otherwise use a large flat fish slice with a long handle.

Clean plates and trays
Essential for cooked food. Never put cooked meats back in the same plate or dish that they came in. One trick is to line the dish of uncooked meats with clingfilm. While the meat is cooking, remove the clingfilm and you are left with a clean dish for the cooked meat.

Timer
An extremely useful piece of equipment to have at your side when manning the barbecue. Over-cooked meats are never a joy to eat so set the timer and then you can carry on socializing. Timers are particularly useful when the lid is down and you can't see exactly what is going on.

Brushes

Essential for basting meats or vegetables as they cook. Today you can buy heatproof silicon brushes but if you can't get hold of these, just use whatever brushes you have available. If you don't have a brush then try using a bunch of hard herbs such as thyme and rosemary to dip into the marinade and brush over the meat or vegetables. This is just as effective and imparts a delicious flavour at the same time.

Kitchen paper
Essential in order to keep your workspace clean. It is also useful to help absorb any meat juices when meat is resting.

Large kitchen knife
This is useful for carving large cuts of meat such as a fillet of beef or a whole chicken.

Small sharp knife

Use this to test if the meat is ready. This is particularly important for pork and chicken, where bacteria are more likely to be found and the temperature is more critical.

Thermometer

This enables you to test if your meat has reached the correct temperature (see "Food safety and hygiene", page 11).

Long matches or lighters

These enable you to light the barbecue easily without burning your fingers.

Chopping boards

Do not use the same boards for cooked and uncooked meats.

Wooden or bamboo skewers

These should be soaked in cold water for at least 30 minutes before cooking so they don't burn. If you have forgotten to soak your skewers then wrap the ends in foil to prevent burning. Alternatively, use metal skewers for long-cooking foods like a whole peri-peri chicken or use sugar cane, rosemary skewers or lemongrass stalks for short-cooking foods such as fish kebabs.

Poultry shears

Useful for cutting through raw chicken with bones.

Hinged wire grills

These are an easy way to cook fish over charcoal. The fish is encased, so you don't have to worry about keeping it intact while turning it.

Drip pan

Use disposable aluminium trays or an old roasting dish that you don't mind ruining. Place it over the coals and under the grill when barbecuing particularly fatty meats or meats in marinades that contain a lot of oil. It will catch the drips and help prevent flaring and burning.

Smoke chip box

Various kinds of smoke chip box are available, from stainless steel to cast iron to makeshift foil packages. They fit inside gas grills, slowly dispersing smoke throughout the cooking process. Cast iron ones, although the most costly, are the most successful at maintaining heat and are the easiest to "top up" as the chips burn out. To make a foil smoker pouch for a gas grill, place soaked wood chips in the centre of a heavy-duty sheet of foil. Fold the edges together to make a tight seal and flatten the package like an envelope. Using the end of a knife, poke several holes in the top of the package to allow the smoke to escape. Place the pouch directly over the burners, under the grill bars. Heat the grill to hot until smoke appears, then adjust to the desired temperature. For charcoal grills, use a grill box or simply scatter soaked chips over the coals.

Heavy-duty oven mitts
Particularly useful when you are dealing with griddle pans on the barbecue or drip pans, which may need to be moved around while still very hot.

BARBECUE INFO
Make sure you have a level site for your barbecue, away from any overhanging trees, and never leave a lit barbecue unattended. Heat the barbecue in advance and rub the grill with a little oil before cooking. Gas barbecues generally take about 10 minutes to get up to temperature, whereas charcoal barbecues take about 30 minutes to reach the required temperature and for the smoke to die down. Indoor griddle pans take about 5 minutes to come up to temperature. See "Getting the temperature right", page 18, to ensure that you are cooking over the correct temperature. Choosing the right barbecue is a very personal choice. Make sure you shop around and find the best deal. Here are a few pointers, which may make your decision a little easier, but ultimately your choice will be dictated by the space you have available and the taste you are after:

Gas barbecues

These are usually the choice of the city dweller who can't be bothered dealing with the mess of charcoal and just wants to light the barbecue at the flick of a switch. The advantage of gas barbecues is that they almost always come with a fold-down lid, which means the barbecue can work like a conventional oven as well as a traditional barbecue. This is useful for cooking more stubborn joints such as chicken drumsticks and whole legs of lamb. A gas barbecue also gives you more control over temperature than a charcoal one. Choose one with both a grill plate and a hot plate so you can cook several meats and vegetables at the same time. Cleaning is also quick and easy in comparison to charcoal models.

Charcoal barbecues

Some people just love getting their hands dirty, and the sight of real flames cooking their food with the smell of charcoal is enough to keep them from converting to gas. There are several types of charcoal barbecue available on the market. The first, and cheapest, is the disposable barbecue. These are readily available in supermarkets and are suitable for one-off uses like picnics and camping. They consist of a foil

container filled with charcoal and topped with a fuel-soaked pad and mesh wiring. They are easy to light and are usually ready to cook on in about 20 minutes. It is important to keep your food moving, as heat cannot be controlled. This applies also to the simple fire box or stand barbecues. Occasionally they will have the added advantage of a moveable grilling rack to lower the food if liked. These barbecues usually have the disadvantage of no air vents for controlling heat.

The kettle barbecue is more advanced and usually comes with controllable air vents, moveable racks and a lid. It acts in the same fashion as a conventional oven. Kettle barbecues are usually made of steel, with a porcelain-enamelled coating which will stand up to numerous barbecue sessions.

It is worth learning how to tell when your charcoal is ready to cook on. A charcoal barbecue takes about 30 minutes before it is ready but, there can be variations. The coals should be covered with a light grey ash, with a bare glimmer of red glow underneath. Do not start cooking until the flames have died down or you will end up with charred food that is still raw in the centre.

Griddle pans

These are invaluable for year-round indoor grilling and many makes also transfer happily to the barbecue grill rack and oven. Their versatility makes them an essential item in any kitchen. The best griddle pans are made of cast iron. If cooking indoors, they are much easier to handle over gas elements, which makes for greater control over temperature. Never oil your griddle pan while hot but instead lightly oil the food if necessary. Get the extractor fans going and heat your dry pan to very hot before you add the food. To test if the pan is hot enough, splash over a little water; it should evaporate immediately. Sear the food quickly then reduce the heat to the desired cooking temperature (see "Getting the temperature right", page 18). Try not to over-crowd your pan or the heat will dramatically decrease.

CLEANING
Clean your barbecue grill rack using a wire brush and warm soapy water or crumpled foil at the end of long tongs in preparation for your next barbecue.

For a gas barbecue, burn off food by keeping the grill on for an extra 10 minutes and scraping off any burnt-on residue using a wire brush, crumpled foil or a metal scraper.

If you are cooking on a charcoal barbecue take time to empty and clean out the firebox after each use. Always allow the charcoal to go cold naturally rather than immersing it in water, which may damage the base of the barbecue. Cover the barbecue with a lid (if you have one) and close any air vents. Leave overnight and the embers will eventually die. Store away from the damp, dirt and cobwebs when not in use and disconnect the gas if using a gas barbecue.

Indoor griddle pans should never be immediately immersed in cold water as the cast iron might fracture. Allow the pan to cool first, loosen any charred food deposits and wash in plenty of hot soapy water. Always dry your grill pan thoroughly and lightly oil before storing it until the next use.

Getting the temperature right
In all of our recipes we have used consistent terminology in order to help you get the cooking times right. Depending on whether you are cooking over a gas barbecue, a charcoal barbecue or on an indoor griddle pan, the basic principles are the same. You will need to use your own initiative sometimes as every piece of equipment varies. If your barbecue has a moveable rack it is much

easier and quicker to adjust the temperature. Likewise, if you are cooking indoors over gas elements rather than electric elements the temperature can be more quickly adjusted. Light or heat your cooking apparatus according to the manufacturer's directions then adjust it to the right temperature.

Hold your hand over the grill bar, hot plate or griddle pan to test the temperature:
Low – you should be able to keep your hand there indefinitely but still feel warmth. This temperature is useful for holding cooked meat when you are not ready to serve.
Medium – you should be able to hold your hand there for 6–7 seconds. This temperature "cooks" the meat and is generally used for larger cuts and longer cooking recipes.
Medium-hot – you should be able to hold your hand there for 3–4 seconds. This temperature will "sizzle" the food.
Hot – you should be able to hold your hand there for 1 second only. This temperature is useful for food wrapped in banana leaves or foil.
Very hot – this is useful for searing meats such as steak and tuna when a rare centre is desired and very quick cooking applies. Don't hold your hand over at this temperature, it's far too hot.

Handy hints for meat and fish

CHICKEN AND DUCK

To spatchcock a chicken

Place the bird breast-side down on a flat surface. Cut down both sides of the backbone, using poultry shears or sharp kitchen scissors. Discard the backbone and snip about 1 cm (½ in) through the wishbone into the breastbone, turn the bird over and press it down flat. To secure the bird in this flattened position it is sometimes helpful to insert two long metal skewers through the bird. Push one skewer horizontally through the wings and breasts and the other horizontally through the thighs. This also makes it easier to handle and turn the bird while cooking. It is best to start cooking a spatchcocked chicken bone-side down, as the heat will take longer to penetrate through the dense bones. You can spatchcock your chicken a day in advance and leave it prepared and covered in the fridge. The same procedure applies for quail, pheasant, poussin and any other bird.

To butterfly a chicken breast

Place the chicken breast on a flat surface. Hold the breast with one hand and, using a sharp knife, slice through the middle horizontally to cut it almost in half. Open the breast and lay out flat or use as a cavity to stuff the chicken breast. If stuffing the chicken breasts, secure the opening using several cocktail sticks or by wrapping the breast in Parma ham, vine leaves or foil. You can prepare your chicken breasts a day in advance and refrigerate, covered, until needed.

To prepare chicken wings

Cut the wing tips off through the joint, using poultry shears or sharp kitchen scissors. You can prepare the wings in advance and refrigerate until needed.

To speed up the cooking of drumsticks

Always make deep slashes through to the bone, on both sides of the drumstick, using poultry shears, sharp kitchen scissors or a sharp knife. This will ensure even cooking without burning.

To check if chicken is cooked through

Insert a small sharp knife into the thickest part of flesh, right down to the bone. The juices should run clear and not pink. If any juices are pink then continue cooking the chicken a little longer until only clear juices run when a knife is inserted.

To score a duck breast

Hold the breast firmly on a flat surface and, using a sharp knife, cut diagonal slashes, about 2 cm (¾ in) apart, through the skin to make a diamond pattern. Ensure that you do not cut right through the skin to the flesh or you will lose all the succulent juices during cooking and the skin will not achieve the desired crispiness.

RED MEAT AND PORK
To butterfly a leg of lamb

Put the lamb on a flat surface, skin-side down, and at the wide end of the leg cut around the exposed bone using a sharp, small knife. Cut a slit along the length of the bone to expose it and, using short, shallow cuts and scrapes, ease the bone away from the meat, trying to lose as little meat as possible. Remove the bone and discard. Hold the meat securely on a flat surface and, with the knife, make a lengthways slit through the two thicker parts of the meat, either side of where the bone was, and open out flat. The butterflied lamb can now be cooked flat or

stuffed and rolled. Always secure your stuffed or rolled lamb using kitchen twine or long metal skewers. Alternatively, ask your butcher to do this for you.

To cook the perfect steak

Heat your griddle pan or barbecue to very hot. Lightly brush your steak with a little oil to stop it sticking. Cook your steak, pressing down slightly with a fish slice to ensure that the whole surface comes in contact with the pan and only turn your steak once! Always rest your steak for a couple of minutes before serving.

To cook steak to your desired doneness

For a 225 g (8 oz) steak cook for 1½ minutes on each side for a rare and very pink steak. It should be rare but warm all the way through. For medium-rare cook for 2½–3 minutes on each side. For medium to well done cook for 3–5 minutes on each side or until cooked through.

To cook sausages

Remember these three golden rules:
– Cook sausages slowly to ensure that the skin doesn't burst.
– Never prick a good-quality sausage, as the casing helps to retain moisture.
– Cut the links between the

sausages cleanly with a sharp knife. When cooked, a sausage should be cooked right through but still juicy and succulent and not charred.

To prevent sausages from burning on the barbecue

Pre-cook or poach the sausages in water before barbecuing. To pre-cook sausages put them in barely simmering water and poach for 20–30 minutes. Be careful not to cook them too fast or the skins will burst. Barbecue or griddle a pre-cooked sausage for 5–10 minutes over medium-hot heat. This will heat the sausages through giving them colour and a smoky flavour.

FISH AND SHELLFISH
To de-sand shellfish

Put the shellfish in a large bowl or bucket of seawater. Add a large handful of oats or flour and leave overnight. The sand will be sitting in the bottom in the morning. Always leave the bucket in a cool place, preferably outside.

To remove bones from salmon

Use sterilized tweezers or pin-nosed pliers. The bones running in a line just off the centre of the spine are called pin bones. For a boneless fillet, pull the bones out at the same angle at which they lie.

To open shellfish without cooking or shucking

Simply put them in the freezer in a single layer for about 1 hour. They will pop open and you will easily be able to remove the top shell.

To deal with a live crayfish

Choose one of the following methods. Plunge the crayfish in boiling water for about 2 minutes. Be careful, as it will try to kick and water may splash. Alternatively, place the crayfish in cold fresh water and it will eventually drown. If you have a sharp knife, and a strong arm, hold the crayfish securely on a flat surface and cut between the eyes – the crayfish will die immediately. Finally, you could place the crayfish in the freezer until it no longer moves.

To cut a crayfish in half

Place it belly-side down and insert a large knife into the cross mark right behind the head, then cut through the head. Turn the crayfish around and, holding it firmly, cut it in half right through the head to the tail.

To test if fish is cooked

Press the fish using your finger or a fork. The fish should "give" and just start to flake apart in the centre.

Starters

Asparagus on horseback

16 asparagus spears
8 slices prosciutto
olive oil spray
extra virgin olive oil

Serves 4

1. Trim the asparagus spears – the best point to break them is where the spears turn pale. Cut prosciutto slices in half and wrap each half around an asparagus spear, starting from the bottom and winding up to the top. Refrigerate until ready to use.

2. Spray the prosciutto-wrapped asparagus lightly with oil and put on the barbecue. Turn constantly for a minute or two, until the prosciutto starts to go crisp and pale.

3. Place the prosciutto-wrapped asparagus on a platter and drizzle over a very small amount of extra virgin olive oil; sprinkle over cracked pepper if you like. You can serve standing around the barbecue area or at the table.

Chicken koftas

500 g/1 lb chicken, finely minced

1 medium onion, finely chopped

1 medium green chilli, seeded and chopped

2 oz fresh mint, chopped

½ tsp salt

1 tsp garam másala

½ tsp ground coriander

½ tsp ground cumin

60 g/2 oz dried breadcrumbs

bamboo skewers, soaked in water for 30 minutes before using mint sprigs, for garnish

Serves 4

1. Combine chicken with onion, chilli, mint, salt, garam masala, coriander, cumin and breadcrumbs. Knead mixture until stiff and smooth and shape into a small sausage around one end of each bamboo skewer. (The meat mixture should be about 2.5 cm/ 1 in in diameter and 7.5 cm/3 in long.) Lay the koftas on a plate lined with plastic wrap, cover and refrigerate for one hour.

2. Spray the koftas with oil and cook on the flat plate for 9 minutes, turning every minute.

3. Arrange on a platter and decorate with mint sprigs.

Crispy focaccia with spicy black-eye bean paste and rocket salad

2 good-sized pieces focaccia

100 g/4 oz rocket leaves

garlic spray oil

140 g/5 oz Spicy black-eye bean paste (*see recipe page 293*)

140 g/5 oz red pepper, diced

70 g/2½ oz sun-dried tomatoes, roughly chopped

35 g/1¼ oz Romano cheese, roughly grated/sliced

extra virgin olive oil

cracked lemon pepper

Serves 4

1. Cut the focaccia through the middle to give 4 even squares or rectangles. Make sure the rocket is washed and crisp.

2. Spray the focaccia with garlic oil, and brown and crisp both sides on the open slats.

3. Spread the cut sides of the focaccia thickly with the Spicy black-eye bean paste. Heap rocket leaves on top of the paste – don't worry if some of them slip off. Sprinkle equal quantities of capsicum, sun-dried tomato and cheese over the top, then drizzle over a little oil and finish off with a sprinkle of pepper. Serve immediately.

Tiny sausages with red pepper sauce

16 tiny sausages/chipolatas

150 ml/5 fl oz Red pepper sauce (*see* page 272), to serve

Serves 4

1. Separate the sausages. Cook the tiny sausages on the open grill, turning every minute, for 3–4 minutes. Lift onto paper towels and drain for 1 minute before serving.

2. Serve the sausages on a warm platter with a bowl of the sauce.

Peaches wrapped in prosciutto

2 peaches

8 pieces very thinly sliced prosciutto

16 small, cocktail sized skewers, soaked for 30 minutes if wooden

Olive oil, for brushing

Makes 16 individual skewers

1. Preheat grill or griddle pan to medium heat.

2. Cut peaches in half, remove stones, then cut each half into fours. Place prosciutto on a chopping board and slice each piece in half lengthways. Wrap the peach wedges with prosciutto and place one on the end of each skewer.

3. Brush each wrapped peach with oil and grill for 2–3 minutes per side, until the prosciutto is crispy and the peaches are slightly charred. Remove from the grill and serve immediately.

Meatballs with homemade barbecue sauce

100 g/3 ½ oz couscous

500 g/1 lb lean minced beef

60 g/2 oz salad onions, chopped

1 tsp prepared curry powder

1 tsp chopped oregano

1 egg

250 ml/8 fl oz homemade barbecue sauce (*see* page 273), to serve

Makes 20–24

1. Pour 120 ml/4 fl oz boiling water over the couscous in a bowl, cover and leave for 3 minutes. Fluff with a fork. Add all the remaining ingredients, except the sauce, and mix well using your hands. Roll into balls 2.5 cm/1 in in diameter (about 25 g/1 oz each) and place on a plate lined with plastic food wrap, cover and refrigerate for 2 hours.

2. Spray the flat plate with oil and cook the meatballs, turning every minute, for 6 minutes.

3. Place meatballs on a warm platter and serve with the sauce to one side. Leftover sauce will keep, refrigerated, for 2 weeks.

Curried courgette poppadum stacks

4 medium yellow courgettes

3 Tbsp vegetable oil

1 tsp black mustard seeds

1 Tbsp Indian curry powder

1 red pepper, cheeks only

1 small onion, peeled and diced

olive oil spray

12 small poppadums

salt to taste

120 ml/4 fl oz Indian mango pickle

240 ml/8 fl oz plain yoghurt

Serves 4

1. Trim the courgettes and cut down their centres lengthwise. Cut these halves into half-moon shapes around 2 cm/¾ in long. Pour the oil into a bowl and mix in the mustard seeds and curry powder. Dice the flesh of the pepper and add it with the onion to the oil mixture. Add the courgette and toss to coat. Leave to sit for 1 hour before cooking.

2. Spray both sides of the poppadums liberally with oil and put them on the open slats two at a time. They crisp and sizzle very quickly so be ready to turn them over. Lift and drain them on kitchen paper towel. Tip the courgette mixture onto the flat plate. Allow it cook through, turning regularly. The courgette is cooked when soft but still holding together. Sprinkle with salt to taste.

3. In the centre of each guest's plate, put a little juice from the courgette and then one poppadum. Spoon over some courgette mixture and add another pappadum; spoon over a little more of the courgette and top with a poppadum. Repeat until all 4 plates are complete. Serve with the Indian mango pickle and yoghurt on the side.

Aubergine mash with pork chipolatas

2–3 large aubergines, about 1 kg/2 lb 4oz in total, halved

2–3 Tbsp olive oil

2 cloves garlic, crushed

2 tsp sumac or juice of 1 lemon

1 small handful parsley, chopped

100 ml/3½ fl oz crème fraîche

Salt and freshly ground black pepper

12 pork chipolatas, about 450 g/1 lb in total, or 24–30 small chipolatas or other pork sausages

2 tsp chopped parsley, to serve

Serves 4

1. Brush the cut surface of the aubergines with oil and barbecue or griddle them over low to medium heat for about 20–30 minutes, turning frequently, until soft, mushy and brown, but still holding their shape. Remove the aubergines and cool slightly. Mash the aubergine flesh using a fork. Add the garlic, sumac, parsley, crème fraîche, salt and pepper and mash further until combined. Set aside while you cook the sausages.

2. Preheat the barbecue or griddle pan to medium and cook the sausages for 6–8 minutes, turning frequently, until golden brown and cooked through. Serve the aubergine mash in a bowl, topped with chopped parsley, with the sausages on the side.

Scallops with anchovy sauce

16 scallops, with roe for the anchovy sauce

60 ml/2 fl oz mayonnaise

1 Tbsp freshly squeezed lemon juice

1 Tbsp cold water

4 anchovy fillets, mashed

4 small sprigs dill

Serves 4

1. Remove the black membrane from the side of each scallop. To make the anchovy sauce, combine all the ingredients and process to a smooth consistency.

2. Spray flat plate with oil and cook scallops for 1 minute. Turn and cook for 1½ minutes more.

3. Spoon a small amount of sauce into the base of 16 Chinese spoons or dessert spoons. Place a scallop on top of each spoon and drizzle with a little more sauce. Serve on a platter, with the leftover sauce, with the spoon handles pointing outwards.

Barbecued haloumi with grape salad

250 g/9 oz haloumi cheese
butter
freshly ground black pepper
1 lemon, cut into wedges

For the salad:

3 Tbsp extra virgin olive oil

1 Tbsp verjuice (or white wine)

2 tsp creamy Dijon mustard

½ tsp salt

freshly ground black pepper
  to taste

1 small buttercrunch lettuce,
  leaves washed and dried

20 g/¾ oz mint leaves

1 tsp lemon thyme (or 1 tsp
  thyme and a little grated
  lemon zest)

85 g/3 oz red grapes, halved
  and deseeded

Serves 3–4

1. Cut cheese into 5 mm slices and pat dry with absorbent kitchen paper.

2. Whisk oil, verjuice, mustard, salt and pepper in a bowl. Add lettuce, torn into bite-sized pieces, mint leaves (tear if large), thyme and grapes. Toss and dish immediately onto individual plates. Ensure everyone is ready to eat as soon as the cheese comes off the barbecue.

3. Cook cheese slices in sizzling butter over medium heat on a barbecue hot plate until lightly golden, then turn over carefully and cook on other side. Season cheese with a little black pepper and a squeeze of lemon juice, then dish onto the salads. Serve immediately.

Sardines on sourdough bread

12–18 small sardines, ungutted

2 Tbsp lemon juice

2 Tbsp extra virgin olive oil plus extra to serve

sea salt and freshly ground black pepper

1 tsp chilli flakes

1 clove garlic

To serve:

1 round loaf

sourdough bread

butter

2 lemons, cut into wedges

1 small bunch parsley, chopped

Serves 4–6

1. Make 2–3 shallow slashes in each side of the sardines and set aside in a shallow dish.

2. Combine the lemon juice, olive oil, salt, pepper, chilli flakes and garlic and pour over the sardines, making sure they are well covered. Cover and leave the sardines to marinate for at least 30 minutes, or refrigerate and marinate overnight.

3. Preheat the barbecue to medium-hot and place the sardines flat in a hinged wire rack. You may need to do two batches. Grill the sardines over the coals for 3–4 minutes on each side or until opaque throughout and crispy on the outside. If you don't have a hinged rack, or are not cooking over coals, cook on the grill part of your barbecue instead.

4. Just before serving, slice the bread thinly and butter it. Put one or two slices of buttered bread and a couple of lemon wedges on each plate. Put the sardines on the bread and drizzle with a little olive oil. Sprinkle with parsley and serve immediately.

Pots of gold

6 medium vine-ripened tomatoes, diced and briefly drained

small handful of fresh basil leaves, chopped

sea salt and freshly ground black pepper

lemon juice

extra virgin olive oil

salad leaves (rocket, watercress, red lettuce, sorrel, etc), washed and dried, white wine vinegar

1 baguette (French bread), pide (flat Turkish bread) or ciabatta loaf (slipper-shaped sourdough loaf)

2 large cloves garlic, peeled

small camembert or brie cheeses (1 per person), at room temperature

Serves 4–6

1. Make a simple tomato salad with diced tomatoes, chopped basil and a little salt, black pepper, a few squirts of lemon juice and a good dousing of olive oil.

2. Dress salad leaves with a splash of vinegar, salt, black pepper and a little olive oil.

3. Slice the baguette, pide or ciabatta and toast pieces over a barbecue grill rack. As they are done rub them, one at a time, with a whole garlic clove. Season with a little sea salt, then stack them one on top of the other.

4. When salads and bread are both ready, cook the cheeses. Place them on an oiled grill rack over a medium heat. Cook for about 5 minutes or until lightly coloured, then turn them over carefully and cook on other side for a few minutes until the cheeses feel soft and runny when gently squeezed around the waist. Carefully transfer cheeses to individual serving plates. To eat, make a shallow cut on top of cheese and partially peel back skin. Dunk in bread and go for it! Serve the salads on the side.

Chargrilled baby octopus with mango salsa

20 baby octopus, cleaned and tenderized

2 Tbsp vegetable oil

¼ tsp sea salt

For the salsa:

500 g/1 lb mango flesh, diced into 1 cm/½ in cubes

100 g/4 oz Spanish onion, finely diced

1 large green fruity chilli, deseeded and finely chopped

2 Tbsp orange juice

1 Tbsp orange zest, finely grated

Serves 4

1. Put the octopus in with the oil and salt, toss then let sit for 10 minutes. This eliminates the need to oil the barbecue plate when cooking.

2. Mix the mango, onion, chilli, juice and zest. Sit for 10 minutes.

3. Cook the octopus over high heat on the flat plate. Toss to cook them evenly. The trick is to not overcook them as they go tough – once firm they are ready to go.

4. Put the salsa into the middle of a large plate and place the octopus around it.

Soy-ginger chicken in banana leaf

50 ml/2 fl oz light soy sauce
50 ml/2 fl oz rice wine
1 Tbsp grated fresh ginger
2 Tbsp soft dark brown sugar
4 chicken breasts
2 banana leaves

Makes about 24

1. Place the soy sauce, rice wine, ginger and sugar in a saucepan and bring to the boil. Reduce the heat and simmer for about 5 minutes, or until just slightly thickened. Leave to cool.

2. Cut the chicken into cubes, about 2.5 cm/ 1 in square and put in a shallow dish. Pour the cooled soy mixture over the chicken and leave to marinate for at least 20 minutes or up to 4 hours in the refrigerator, turning once or twice.

3. Just before you are ready to start cooking, wash the banana leaves and use a sharp knife to remove the thick central rib. Cut the leaves into rectangles large enough to enclose one of the cubes of chicken. To prevent the banana leaf from splitting when folded, pass it over a gas flame or put it under an electric grill until it becomes pliable. Put a cube of chicken on each rectangle of banana leaf and fold the leaf over to enclose the chicken completely. Secure the parcel with a wooden cocktail stick.

4. When the parcels are all made, cook them over a hot barbecue for about 8–10 minutes, or until the chicken is cooked, turning once or twice during cooking. Serve immediately. Unwrap the parcels before eating and use the cocktail sticks to pick up the chicken.

Atlantic salmon risotto cakes

500 g/1 lb basic risotto, cooled (see below)

1 Tbsp lemon zest, finely grated

100 g/4 oz Atlantic salmon, boneless, skinless and finely chopped

2 eggs

100 g/4 oz plain flour

1 tsp dill, ground

breadcrumbs

olive oil spray

For the risotto:

30 g/2 oz butter

3 Tbsp onions, finely chopped

2 clove garlic, chopped

1 cup Italian arborio rice

32 fl oz/950 ml boiling fish/prawn stock

3 Tbsp parmesan cheese, finely grated

1 tsp salt

½ tsp white pepper

2 Tbsp dill, finely chopped

Serves 4

1. Melt butter in a large heavy saucepan and fry onion and garlic until soft and golden. Stir in the rice and cook for 3 minutes, stirring constantly, then add 1 cup boiling stock stirring until it is absorbed. Add stock a cupful at a time and stir constantly, for 15–20 minutes or until rice is tender and all liquid is absorbed—the risotto should be creamy and white.

2. Stir in cheese, salt, pepper and dill.

3. Mix the room temperature or chilled risotto with the zest, salmon, eggs, flour and dill—stir well. Divide the risotto into 24 equal portions and roll into balls. Flatten into rounds of 4cm in diameter and 2cm thick, then coat in breadcrumbs. Make sure all excess breadcrumbs are removed. Refrigerate until ready to use.

4. Spray the flat plate liberally with oil, add the cakes and cook for 1 minute. Spray liberally with oil, turn and cook for another minute on the other flat side. Serve as a 'pass around' or place in the middle of the table. A tossed salad served with them makes more of an appetiser.

Trout brochettes with satay dipping sauce

16 x 30 g/2 oz pieces trout, skinless and bones removed

16 small bamboo or stainless steel skewers (the larger, longer toothpicks are good)

vegetable oil spray

4 fl oz/120 ml thick satay sauce

2 fl oz/60 ml coconut cream

coriander leaves for decoration

Serves 4

1. Thread one piece of the fish onto the tip of each skewer – refrigerate until ready to cook.

2. Heat the satay sauce and coconut cream until warmed and combined then pour into dipping bowl.

3. Spray the trout with a little oil (remembering that this fish has naturally good oil in it) and cook on a medium–hot flat plate for 30 seconds each side. Serve on a plate with the dipping sauce in the middle and decorated with coriander leaves.

Butterflied prawns served with chilli jam

12 medium-size raw tiger
prawns, peeled and
deveined with tails left on

2 Tbsp chilli jam
(*see* page 282), to serve

Serves 4

1. Butterfly the prawns by slicing down the
back of each prawn from the head end to
the tail. (Leave the tails on the prawns as it
helps to hold them together.) Make sure you
don't cut right through to the stomach. Open
out the prawn, so that it resembles a butterfly,
and flatten the flesh gently. Take care as the
flesh is very delicate.

2. Spray prawns with oil and cook on the flat
plate for 30 seconds. Turn and cook for
30 seconds longer.

3. Warm the chilli jam and spoon some into
the centre of each plate. Place 3 cooked
prawns on each plate.

Sesame tuna with marinated cucumber

1 tuna fillet, about 750 g–1 kg/
  1 lb 10 oz–2 lb 4 oz

1 Tbsp sesame oil

4 Tbsp black sesame seeds

4 Tbsp white sesame seeds

For the cucumber salad:

1 cucumber

salt and freshly ground black
  pepper

juice of 2 lemons

2 Tbsp extra virgin olive oil

To serve:

lemon wedges

wasabi (optional)

Serves 4–6

1. Pat the tuna dry and cut into thick batons approximately 5 cm/2 in wide and 2 cm/¾ in thick. Rub the sesame oil evenly over the tuna batons.

2. In a large shallow dish or tray combine the sesame seeds and roll the tuna in the seeds, coating it evenly. Put the tuna in a clean dish, cover and refrigerate until you are ready to cook.

3. To prepare the cucumber salad, slice the unpeeled cucumber, using a floating blade vegetable peeler to give you long strips. Work your way around the cucumber but try to avoid too many seeds if you can. Put the cucumber in a bowl with the salt, pepper, lemon juice and olive oil. Mix well and leave to marinate for at least 30 minutes.

4. Preheat the barbecue hot plate or griddle pan to hot and sear the tuna batons on each side for about 30 seconds to 1 minute then remove from the pan and allow to rest for 5 minutes. Cut the tuna into 1 cm/½ in thick slices and serve with the cucumber salad, lemon wedges and wasabi on the side.

Mediterranean stuffed squid

4–6 large squid about 500 g/1 lb in total

150 g/5¼ oz fresh breadcrumbs

1 chilli, deseeded and finely chopped

1 handful oregano, chopped

1 handful parsley, chopped

Grated rind of 1 lemon

1 clove garlic, crushed

2 Tbsp olive oil plus extra for cooking

½ tsp salt

Salt and freshly ground black pepper

Lemons cut into wedges, to serve

Serves 4–6

1. Wash the squid and pull the tentacles out from the body. Discard the transparent quill if it is still there and rinse the inside of the squid. Pat dry using kitchen paper.

2. Put the breadcrumbs, chilli, herbs, lemon rind, garlic, 2 Tbsp oil and ½ tsp salt in a food processor and process for about 1 minute, or until the mixture comes together slightly but is still coarse. Loosely pack the stuffing into the squid bodies, ensuring that you do not stuff them completely full. Secure the ends using cocktail sticks. When all the squid are stuffed, drizzle over a little extra oil and season with salt and pepper.

3. Preheat the barbecue or griddle pan to medium-hot and cook the squid for about 2–3 minutes on each side, or until the flesh sets white and is firm. Slice the squid into about 4–5 pieces and serve hot with lemon wedges on the side.

Meat

Chicken and barbecued corn salsa

4 medium-sized chicken breasts, boneless

1 large corn cob, husk and silk removed

100 g/3½ oz tomatoes, unpeeled, cooked and diced

100 g/3½ oz mango flesh, diced

1 very small red onion, peeled and finely diced

1 small banana chilli, deseeded and minced

1 Tbsp parsley, chopped

salt and ground black pepper to taste

2 Tbsp sherry vinegar

3 Tbsp olive oil

olive oil spray

20 asparagus tips

Serves 4

1. Slice each chicken breast, on the diagonal, into 3 evenly-sized slices and flatten slightly. When the cooked corn (see below) is cool enough to handle, cut the kernels from the cob into a bowl. Add the tomatoes, mango, onion, chilli, parsley, salt and pepper. Stir in the vinegar and oil.

2. Spray the corn cob with oil and cook on the open slats, turning regularly to lightly brown the corn. When done, return it to the kitchen to become part of the salsa. Put the asparagus tips onto the barbecue and lightly cook. Spray the sliced chicken well with the oil. Place slices on the flat plate, turning to seal both sides. Transfer chicken to the open slats to cook through for approximately 2–3 minutes on each side.

3. Spoon equal amounts of salsa onto each guest's plate and top with 3 chicken slices. Place asparagus tips on top of the chicken and serve.

Duck quesadillas

750 g/1½ lb boneless
   duck breasts

60 g/3 oz Jalapeño chillies,
   sliced

60 g/3 oz onion, finely
   chopped

60 g/3 oz coriander
   leaves, rinsed

salt and pepper to taste

8 medium-sized flour tortillas

230 g/8 oz Cheddar cheese,
   grated

olive oil spray

Semi-roasted tomato salsa
   (*see* page 288)

Serves 4

1. Trim the duck breasts of as much fat as possible. Mix the chillies, onion, coriander leaves, salt and pepper together. Make the salsa.

2. Put duck breasts on the open slats on medium-high, skin side down. Allow duck to brown very well, about 2 minutes, then turn and cook for 5–7 minutes. Turn duck again and cook on the skin side for 2 minutes. Remove and let rest for 5 minutes. When cool enough to handle, slice duck into very thin strips. To make quesadillas, lay a flour tortilla out flat and spoon a quarter of the cheese over half of it. Add some duck slices and then some of the chilli mix. Fold tortilla over the stuffing, tuck the edge in under the filling and set aside. Repeat until all tortillas are filled.

3. Spray the flat plate with oil and add the quesadillas, folded side up, and allow to cook for 1–2 minutes. Spray the quesadilla with oil and flip it over quickly, holding the top as you do to stop the filling from falling out. The cheese should have melted enough to grip most of the filling. Cook quesadillas for about 2 minutes on the second side and lift off the plate when done.

4. Serve the quesadillas on a large platter in the centre of the table, with the salsa on the side.

Quail on pineapple-scented couscous

4 large quails

60 ml/2 fl oz olive oil plus
   1 Tbsp extra

4 x 2 cm/1 in thick slices
   fresh pineapple

1 small red onion, peeled

340 g/12 oz dried couscous

450 g/16 fl oz boiling water

60 g/2 oz basil leaves

60 g/2 oz mint leaves

1 tsp Baharat spice

sea salt and powdered black pepper

2 Tbsp toasted sesame seeds

Serves 4

1. Cut the quail into quarters. Remove the winglets and place the quarters in a bowl; drizzle over the 60 ml/2 fl oz of olive oil, toss to coat the quail and refrigerate until ready for use. Cut the pineapple slices into half moons and remove the core. Finely dice the onion.

2. Put the couscous in a bowl and pour over boiling water. Leave for 30 seconds then add the diced onion and the tablespoon of olive oil; fork these through to stop the grains sticking together.

3. Cut the browned pineapple slices (see below) into small wedges and mix with the basil and mint leaves. Add the Baharat spice, salt and pepper and toss to combine the flavours. Allow to sit for a minute, then add to the couscous and fold in to meld the flavours.

4. Remove the quail from the refrigerator 10 minutes before use and drain off the oil. Place on the barbecue, turn regularly and cook until done (about 2–3 minutes on each side). Remove when done and keep warm; quail tends to dry out when it is over-cooked. Sprinkle over the sesame seeds and toss to coat the quail pieces.

5. Flash-cook the pineapple slices by placing them on the open slats and turning them often until the slices brown slightly. When done, remove and return them to the kitchen.

6. Place the couscous mixture on a large platter, arrange the pieces of quail on top and serve.

Barbecued pork and green apple salad

400 g/14 oz pork fillet

2 medium green apples or green mangoes

½ tsp salt

olive oil spray

3 cloves garlic, sliced

4 green spring onions, trimmed and sliced diagonally

1 Tbsp fish sauce (Nam Pla)

3 Tbsp roasted peanuts, crushed

1 tsp palm sugar

½ tsp ground white pepper

1 large green chilli, deseeded and finely sliced

Serves 4

1. Trim the pork to make sure all fat and silver tissue is removed. If using apples, core and quarter them, then slice very finely. If using mangoes, peel off the skin and slice the flesh from the seed, then cut very finely into batons. Place the slices of fruit in a bowl, sprinkle with salt and toss.

2. Spray the pork fillets with oil and put on the flat plate. Roll the fillets so they are sealed on all sides, then transfer to the open slats to cook through; be careful not to overcook the pork. When cooked, remove to rest for 5 minutes before slicing. Spray the flat plate with oil and toss on the garlic and spring onion slices for 1 minute, then remove and set aside.

3. Slice the pork finely into 1–2 cm/½–1 in thick rounds and halve if large slices. Add pork slices to the apples (or mangoes) and add the other ingredients except for the chilli. Toss salad gently and then sprinkle the sliced chilli over the top.

Beef fajitas

500 g/1 lb rump steak

2 Tbsp of light olive oil

2 Tbsp red wine vinegar

½ Tbsp ground allspice

½ Tbsp oregano, dried and ground

2 Tbsp dried onion flakes

1 tsp salt

¼ tsp chilli powder

8 wheat flour tortillas

olive oil spray

60 g/2 oz lettuce, shredded

60 g/2 oz carrot, grated

2 medium-sized salad tomatoes, cut into wedges

120 ml/4 fl oz sour cream

Serves 4

1. Cut the steak across the grain into strips 1 cm/½ in wide and place in bowl. Mix together the oil, vinegar, allspice, oregano, onion flakes, salt, and chilli powder, and pour over the steak strips. Stir so all pieces are coated, cover and refrigerate for at least 2 hours.

2. Tip the strips onto the flat plate and spread them out over it. Cook steak by tossing and lifting the strips and allowing them to brown. The steak will cook in 5–6 minutes; remove when done. Spray the tortillas with oil and heat very quickly on the open slats for 30 seconds each side. Remove them and keep them warm.

3. Serve the steak strips on a platter in the centre of the table, surrounded by the lettuce, carrots, tomatoes, tortillas and sour cream on separate platters. Assemble the fajitas by placing some lettuce on each tortilla, then some carrot and steak strips, topped with sour cream. Add some tomato wedges. To eat, roll up the fajitas or fold them, whichever is easier.

Lamb cutlets saltimbocca with pea and tomato linguine

8–12 trimmed lamb cutlets, depending on size and appetite

8–12 large sage leaves

8–12 thin slices Parmesan cheese

8–12 slices prosciutto

2 Tbsp olive oil

500 g/1 lb cooked and oiled linguine

120 g/4 oz peas, fresh or frozen

2 medium-sized ripe tomatoes, diced

2 Tbsp tomato sauce for pasta

60 ml/2 fl oz lamb or beef stock

sea salt and ground black pepper

Serves 4

1. On top of each cutlet, place a sage leaf, then enough Parmesan cheese to cover both sage and cutlet. Wrap in a slice of prosciutto and set aside. Repeat with the remaining cutlets. Just before the lamb is ready to come off the barbecue (see below), heat olive oil in a suitable pan over medium heat. Add the linguine, peas, tomatoes and tomato sauce. Stir, then pour in the stock so that the peas and tomatoes cook and provide a good sauce for the linguine. Season with salt and pepper.

2. Cook the lamb cutlets on the flat plate, turning regularly. When the cheese starts to seep through the crisped prosciutto, the cutlets are ready. Immediately transfer the cutlets to a platter.

3. Serve the cutlets on a platter and the linguine in a large bowl. A garden salad goes well with this dish.

Pepper-crusted lamb rump with lentil, peas and mint salad

4 lamb rumps

cracked black pepper

200 g/7 oz dried green lentils

1 large onion, roughly chopped

200 g/7 oz sugar snap peas

200 g/7 oz peas

2 eggs, for omelettes

2 Tbsp parsley, finely chopped

olive oil spray

120 g/4 oz mint leaves, torn

120 ml/4 fl oz olive oil

60 ml/2 fl oz lemon juice (from the lemons used for the cheeks)

sea salt to taste

4 lemon cheeks

Serves 4

1. Trim the rumps of all fat and roll them in as much or as little cracked black pepper as you like. Refrigerate until ready to use. Soak the lentils in cold water for 20 minutes. Drain and put into a saucepan with the onion. Cover well with water, bring to the boil then simmer until the lentils are soft – about 30–40 minutes. Drain and rinse the lentils under cold water. Blanch the sugar snap peas and the peas.

2. Make a 1-egg omelette by beating 1 egg with 1 tablespoon of water and 1 tablespoon of parsley. Pour the mixture into a non-stick small pan and let it run all over the base. The omelette should be very thin and resemble a crepe. When set, flip over, leave for 15 seconds then slide out of the pan. Repeat for the other omelette. When cooked and cooled, roll them into a sausage shape and cut into strips ½ cm/¼ in wide.

3. Assemble the salad by combining the lentils and onion, peas, sliced omelettes and mint. Toss with the oil, lemon juice and salt.

4. Spray the flat plate well with oil and put the lamb rumps on. Cook for 2 minutes on each side, then cover with a wok lid or stainless steel bowl. Cook for up to 4–5 minutes on each side, then let rest for 10 minutes before slicing. Place the lemon cheeks on the open slats cut-side down for 1 minute before serving the lamb. Serve the lamb on individual plates. Slice each rump into 4 slices and place on the plate with a lemon cheek to one side.

Steak sandwiches with fennel relish

For the fennel relish:

1 Tbsp extra virgin olive oil

1 onion, thinly sliced

1 large fennel bulb, very thinly sliced

1 clove garlic, crushed

4 Tbsp caster sugar

1 Tbsp wholegrain mustard

2 Tbsp white wine vinegar or cider vinegar

4 sirloin steaks about 1.5 cm/¾ in thick

Salt and freshly ground black pepper

8 slices sourdough bread, griddled

Rocket leaves

Rosemary aïoli (see page *292*) (optional)

Serves 4

1 First make the fennel relish. Heat the oil in a non-stick saucepan over medium heat and add the onion, fennel and garlic. Stir until well coated in the oil and the onion and fennel start to soften but not brown. Increase the heat, add the sugar and stir constantly for a further 2–3 minutes, or until starting to brown. Stir in the mustard and vinegar and season generously with salt and pepper. When the liquid has evaporated, reduce the heat slightly and leave the mixture to caramelize and darken around the edges, stirring occasionally, for a further 8–12 minutes. Cool.

2. Preheat the barbecue or griddle pan to very hot. Season the steak generously on both sides and sear for 2–3 minutes on each side or until cooked to your taste. Lay 2 slices of sourdough bread on each of 4 serving plates. Place relish on one piece, top with a steak, aïoli (if using) and rocket, season generously, then top with the second slice of bread. Serve immediately.

Peri-peri spatchcocked chicken

1 medium chicken, about 1.3 kg/3 lb, spatchcocked (*see* page 19)

2–3 red chilli peppers, stems removed and roughly chopped

juice of 2 lemons, about 4 Tbsp

4 Tbsp olive oil

1 Tbsp cayenne pepper

2 cloves garlic, crushed

1 Tbsp smoked paprika

1 tsp salt

Serves 4

1. Spatchcock the chicken. Insert a metal skewer horizontally through the wings and breast. Push a second metal skewer horizontally through the thighs. Set aside until the marinade is ready.

2. Put the chilli peppers, lemon juice, oil, cayenne, garlic, paprika and salt in a food processor or blender and process to a smooth paste. Place half the marinade in a large flat dish. Put the chicken on top and pour over the remaining marinade, ensuring that it covers both sides. Cover and refrigerate for at least 30 minutes or up to 24 hours.

3. Preheat the barbecue to hot. Cook, bone-side down for 15–20 minutes, reducing the heat if necessary. Turn the chicken over and cook skin-side down for a further 15–20 minutes, depending on the size of the bird, or until the skin is brown and crispy but not burned. Cook until no pink juices run from the meat when a skewer is inserted into the thigh. When the bird is cooked leave it to rest, covered, for 5 minutes. Cut into four and serve.

Five-spice roasted and grilled pork belly

2 Tbsp Chinese 5-spice powder

2 tsp grated fresh ginger

2 cloves garlic, crushed

2 Tbsp fish sauce

1 Tbsp lemon juice

100 g/3½ oz brown sugar

400 g/14 oz tin chopped tomatoes

2 Tbsp tomato purée

1.5–2 kg/3 lb 5 oz piece pork belly, bones removed, rind on and slashed

Gran's plum sauce (*see* page 275) and grilled cherry tomatoes, to serve

Serves 4–6

1. To make the marinade, put all the ingredients (except the pork, plum sauce and cherry tomatoes) in a food processor and purée until smooth. Pour it all over and under the pork, ensuring that you spread it into the slashes. Cover, refrigerate and leave the meat to marinate for 1–2 hours. Preheat the oven to 180° C/350° F (gas 4). Line a roasting tray with foil and sit a rack that is large enough to hold the pork in the centre. Place the pork, rind-side down, on the rack and cook towards the top of the oven for 30 minutes. After 30 minutes, baste the pork all over with more marinade. Cook for a further 45 minutes–1 hour, basting every 20 minutes. Turn the meat rind side up, baste and cook for a further 30 minutes. Remove from the oven and allow to cool.

2. Once cool, slice the pork into ½–1 cm/¼–½ in slices. Cook on a hot barbecue or griddle pan for 1–2 minutes on each side, or until crispy and charred. The fat may spit so be careful. Serve hot, with Gran's Plum Sauce and grilled cherry tomatoes.

Flatbreads with lamb and tzatziki

Flatbread dough
  (*see* page 297)

4 lamb leg steaks

**salt and freshly ground black
  pepper, to taste**

**100 g/3½ oz mixed salad
  leaves**

Tzatziki (*see* page 279)

Serves 4

1. Prepare the flatbread dough as directed (*see* page 297).

2. Preheat the barbecue or a large griddle pan to very hot. Season and cook the lamb steaks for 3–4 minutes on each side, or until cooked to your taste. Set aside to rest.

3. Wipe down the pan or barbecue before cooking the flatbreads. Cook the flatbreads as directed (see page 297). Continue until all the flatbreads are cooked, stacking on top of each other and covering with a tea towel to keep them warm and soften them.

4. Slice the lamb steaks and lay some meat, salad leaves and Tzatziki on half of each flatbread then fold in half to eat.

Top loin with chimichurri marinade

250 ml/8 fl oz extra virgin olive oil

2 Tbsp chopped thyme

2 Tbsp chopped oregano

2 Tbsp chopped flat-leaf parsley

1 Tbsp chopped rosemary

1 chipotle chilli in adobo sauce, chopped

1 Tbsp sweet Spanish paprika

3 cloves garlic, finely chopped

3 Tbsp red wine vinegar

½ tsp sea salt

freshly ground black pepper

600 g/1 lb 5 oz top sirloin steak about 2.5 cm/1¼ in thick

Serves 2

1. Heat the olive oil in a medium-sized saucepan until hot. Remove from the heat and set aside. Add the remaining ingredients, except for the steak, stir, and leave at room temperature to cool and infuse for 1 hour.

2. Pour one quarter of this marinade into a dish and add the steak, turning several times to coat. Reserve the remaining marinade to serve with the cooked steak. Cover and refrigerate for 1 hour. Remove and leave at room temperature for 30 minutes.

3. Preheat the barbecue or griddle pan to very hot and cook the steak for 2 minutes on each side for medium-rare. Transfer the steak to a chopping board and loosely cover with foil. Allow it to rest for 5 minutes before thinly slicing across the grain. Serve with the reserved marinade.

Veal cutlets with olive, parsley & lime pesto

4 x 200 g/7 oz veal cutlets

olive, parsley and lime pesto

20 green olives, seeds removed

2 limes, grated zest only

juice of one of the limes

2 cloves garlic, peeled and halved

1 Tbsp pine nuts

250 g/8 oz tightly packed flat parsley

75 ml/2½ fl oz extra virgin olive oil

400 g/14 oz waxy potatoes

olive oil spray

fresh oregano, chopped

sea salt and ground black pepper

Serves 4

1. Trim the veal cutlets if necessary, cover with cling wrap and refrigerate until ready to use. Put the olives, lime zest, lime juice, garlic, pine nuts and parsley in a food processor bowl and start the motor. Gradually pour in the olive oil and work until combined. The mixture will be roughly chopped when you remove it from the processor bowl; cover and refrigerate. Wash potatoes and peel, if desired; if potatoes are large, cut into halves or quarters. Boil potatoes for 3 minutes, then drain and cool.

Refrigerate until ready to use. Remove veal and potatoes from the refrigerator 15 minutes before use.

2. Spray the cutlets with plenty of oil and place on hot barbecue. Leave for a minute to seal, then turn and seal the other side for a minute. Move cutlets to medium heat and cook them to your liking. Sprinkle on some oregano and press into each cutlet with the back of the cooking spatula. Turn cutlets only one more time and repeat the oregano on the other side. Sprinkle with salt and pepper on the second turning only – do not put on raw meat. Spray the potatoes well and put on to medium heat. Sprinkle with salt and pepper and turn regularly until browned, crisp and cooked through.

3. Transfer veal cutlets from the barbecue to a plate and let them rest for 3 minutes. Place potato in the centre of each plate and top with the veal cutlets. Spoon some of the pesto over the cutlets and put the remainder on the table.

Butterflied Thai coconut chicken breasts

2 Tbsp Sweet Thai chilli sauce (*see* page 274)

grated rind and juice of 1 lime

1 Tbsp fish sauce

2 tsp grated fresh ginger

10 g/¼ oz coriander, roughly chopped

150 ml/5 fl oz coconut milk

4 chicken breasts, butterflied (*see* page 19)

Serves 4

1. Combine all the ingredients, except the chicken breasts, in a bowl. Put a third of this marinade in a flat dish, place the butterflied chicken breasts on top and pour over the remaining marinade, ensuring that it covers all the chicken. Leave the chicken to marinate in the refrigerator for at least 2 hours or up to 24 hours.

2. Preheat the barbecue or griddle pan to medium and cook the chicken for 3–4 minutes on the first side, turn, and cook for a further 2–3 minutes or until cooked through and only clear juices run from the meat. Serve the chicken breasts whole with a side dish of rice and vegetables or chop them into a green salad.

Lime-marinated chicken with peanut sauce

6 chicken thighs, boned and trimmed of all fat

125 ml/4 fl oz freshly squeezed lime juice

3 Kaffir lime leaves, vein removed, finely shredded

1 Tbsp finely chopped fresh ginger

1 large green chilli, seeded and chopped

30 g/1 oz white sugar

1 Tbsp peanut oil

250 ml/8 fl oz peanut sauce (*see* page 276)

8 sprigs fresh coriander

Serves 4

1. Cut chicken thighs in half so you have 12 pieces. Combine the lime juice, lime leaf, ginger, chilli and sugar, stirring well. Pour over the chicken thighs, coating the meat well with the marinade. Cover and refrigerate for 30 minutes.

2. Oil the flat plate with the peanut oil. Remove chicken thighs from the marinade and drain well, reserving marinade. Cook chicken for 2 minutes on each side, basting with reserved marinade. With a sharp knife and a set of tongs, cut the chicken thighs into strips about 1 cm/$\frac{1}{2}$ in wide (on the flat plate). Move the chicken pieces to a central area and pour over half the peanut sauce. Lift and toss the chicken so the sauce coats the pieces. Cook for a total of 9 minutes.

3. Lift the chicken onto a warm platter and pour over the remaining peanut sauce. Garnish with coriander sprigs and serve with boiled rice or boiled vermicelli noodles.

Duck breasts with pak choy and celeriac

4 x 155 g/5 oz Muscovy duck breasts

4 medium-size pak choy (Chinese chard)

220 g/7 oz celeriac

1 Tbsp white vinegar

2 medium shallots, peeled and finely diced

125 ml/4 fl oz basic handmade mayonnaise (*see* page 280)

1 Tbsp Japanese pickled ginger, finely sliced

1 Tbsp pickled ginger juice

Serves 4

1. Trim the duck breasts, if necessary, but leave the skin on – this is essential. Trim, wash and halve the pak choy. Peel and roughly grate the celeriac and sprinkle with white vinegar. Combine celeriac, shallots, mayonnaise, ginger and ginger juice. Stir well and refrigerate, covered, for 1 hour before use.

2. Place duck breasts, skin-side-down, on the open grill and cook for three minutes. Do not move them about as you want good clear grill marks on the skin. Turn duck breasts over where they have been cooking so that the natural fat on the grill will lubricate the bare flesh. Cook for a further 4 minutes, remove from the heat and rest for 5 minutes before slicing.

3. Spray pak choy with oil and place on the barbecue. Cook, turning only once, for 1½ minutes, or until done to your liking. The time may vary, depending on the thickness of the white part of the bok choy. It must remain crunchy.

4. Place two halves of pak choy in the centre of each plate and spoon some celeriac onto them. Slice duck breasts into rounds and sit on top of the celeriac and pak choy.

Caramelized lamb chops

20 g/¾ oz coriander, roughly
  chopped

6 Tbsp brown sugar

4 Tbsp dark soy sauce

4 Tbsp mirin, Chinese rice wine
  or sherry

4 cloves garlic, finely chopped

16 single-rib lamb chops

To serve:

grilled potatoes, green salad
  or steamed green beans

Serves 4

1. Combine the coriander, brown sugar, soy sauce, mirin and garlic in a shallow baking dish. Add the chops, turning well to coat in the marinade. Cover and refrigerate overnight or for up to 24 hours.

2. Preheat the barbecue or griddle pan to very hot. Brush with oil. Grill the chops to taste (4–6 minutes on each side for medium) until the edges are browned and caramelized. Transfer the chops to a platter and allow to rest for 2–3 minutes before serving with grilled potatoes and a green salad or steamed green beans.

Grilled chicken, papaya and chilli salad

450 g/1 lb skinless, boneless chicken breasts or thighs

vegetable oil, for brushing

400 g/14 oz green papaya, finely sliced

4 Tbsp palm or brown sugar

4 Tbsp fish sauce

150 ml/5 fl oz lime or lemon juice

4 cloves garlic

100 g/3½ oz peanuts, roasted

100 g/3½ oz green beans, cut into 2.5 cm/1¼ in lengths

1 red "finger" chilli pepper, chopped (optional)

200 g/7 oz cherry tomatoes, halved

Serves 4–6

1. Preheat the barbecue or griddle pan to medium-hot. Brush the chicken with oil and grill for about 3–4 minutes on each side. Cool then roughly chop.

2. Peel the skin off the papaya, scoop out the seeds and julienne the flesh. In a small bowl, blend the palm sugar, fish sauce and lemon or lime juice until the sugar has dissolved. Using a large pestle and mortar or a food processor, pound the garlic cloves with the roasted peanuts until well smashed. Add the papaya, sugar mixture, green beans and chilli, if using, and gently pound until slightly bruised. Place in a large bowl. Add the cherry tomatoes and chicken and stir until everything is combined. Leave the salad to infuse for 15 minutes before serving.

Blue cheese burgers

500 g/1lb medium-minced beef

1 Tbsp Dijon mustard

3 spring onions, finely chopped

1 clove garlic, crushed

½ tsp salt

½ tsp pepper

Olive oil for brushing

80 g/3 oz blue cheese, sliced into 8 pieces

4 hamburger buns

Suggested toppings:

Mayonnaise (*see* page 280), Caramelized onions (*see* page 296), lettuce leaves

Serves 4

1. In a large bowl, combine the beef with the mustard, spring onions, garlic, salt and pepper. Stir briefly (this is easiest done with your hands), until just combined. Wet your hands and shape the mixture into four burgers, about 125 g/4 oz each. Season the burgers with a sprinkling of salt and pepper.

2. Preheat the barbecue or griddle pan to medium-hot and brush with oil. Grill the burgers until brown and charred, about 5 minutes. Turn over and grill for a further 2 minutes for a medium-rare burger, or a further 3–4 minutes for a medium burger. When the second side is grilling, place two pieces of cheese on each burger. Grill the buns at the same time. When the cheese has melted and the burgers are cooked through, remove from the grill.

3. Serve with your choice of toppings.

Barbecued beef steak stir-fry

500 g/1 lb beef strips, either rump or sirloin

1 tsp ground allspice

60 ml/2 fl oz soy sauce

1 Tbsp mirin

1 Tbsp peanut oil, or vegetable oil

1 medium-size red chilli, seeded and finely chopped

2 coriander roots, washed and finely chopped

1 Tbsp palm sugar (jaggery) or dark brown sugar

1 small onion, cut into wedges

240 g/8 oz bean sprouts

8 water chestnuts, finely sliced

40 g/1½ oz loosely packed coriander leaves

Serves 4

1. Put the meat in a bowl and sprinkle with allspice. Combine soy, mirin, oil, chilli, coriander root and palm sugar. Mix well to dissolve the sugar. Pour over the meat, cover and leave to sit for one hour. Drain the meat, reserving the soy mixture.

2. Spray the flat plate liberally with oil. Add meat strips immediately. Put onions on another part of the sprayed plate and turn both meat and onions regularly for two minutes. Do not combine. Add bean sprouts and water chestnuts to onions; lift and toss to combine all ingredients, including the meat, in a concentrated area on the barbecue. Spoon over some of the reserved marinade and lift and toss for another two minutes. Lift into a serving bowl, add the coriander leaves and toss gently.

3. Serve stir-fry with boiled rice or rice noodles.

Spinach and ricotta-stuffed chicken

1 Tbsp olive oil

1 onion, finely chopped

2 cloves garlic, finely chopped

grated rind of 1 lemon

100 g/3½ oz vacuum-packed chestnuts, crumbled

salt and freshly ground black pepper

225 g/8 oz spinach leaves

100 g/3½ oz ricotta or quark

4–6 chicken breasts

8–12 slices Parma ham

green salad, to serve

Serves 4–6

1. Heat the oil in a large frying pan. Add the onion and sauté for 2–3 minutes, or until translucent. Add the garlic, lemon rind, chestnuts, salt and pepper and sauté for a further 2–3 minutes, or until just starting to brown and the mixture is quite dry. Remove from the heat and cool completely.

2. Cook the spinach in a large saucepan with boiling water until bright green and wilted. Drain and squeeze out any excess water. Cut the spinach finely and set aside. When the chestnut mixture is cool add the spinach and ricotta and mix well. Season. Cut a pocket in each chicken breast and fill with one quarter or one sixth of the mixture, depending on size. Hold the breasts and wrap 2 slices of Parma ham tightly around them.

3. Preheat the barbecue or griddle pan to hot and cook the chicken breasts for 6–8 minutes on each side, reducing the heat to medium after about 2 minutes. Continue until cooked through and no pink juices run from the meat when cut. Allow to rest, covered, for about 5 minutes and serve with a green salad.

Grilled rump and vegetables

3 Tbsp olive oil

3 cloves garlic, peeled and grated

2 tsp ground cumin

1 tsp ground coriander

2 Tbsp lemon juice

2 x 600 g/1¼ lb pieces rump steak, 5cm thick

2 red peppers

2 yellow peppers

18 asparagus spears

1 red onion, peeled and thickly sliced

olive oil for cooking

sea salt

fresh coriander sprigs

Serves 6-8

1. Combine the olive oil, garlic, cumin, coriander and lemon jiuce in a shallow dish. Coat the meat with the marinade, cover and refrigerate overnight.

2. Cut the peppers into four lengthways. Remove the core and seeds, then cut each quarter into half, again lengthways. Snap the hard ends fron the asparagus. Brush the vegetables with olive oil and season with a little sea salt.

3. Grill the beef and vegetables over medium to high heat until the vegetables are lightly charred and tender and the steak medium-rare. Keep the vegetables warm and allow the meat to rest for 5 minutes. Cut the meat into 1cm slices and layer it on a platter with the grilled vegetables. Garnish with the coriander sprigs and serve with crusty bead to mop up the juices.

Pork ribs with mustard bourbon sauce

For the multi-purpose dry rub:
2 Tbsp ground cumin
1 Tbsp chilli powder
1 Tbsp dry mustard powder
1 Tbsp coarse sea salt
1 1/2 tsp cayenne pepper
1 1/2 tsp ground cardamom
1 1/2 tsp ground cinnamon

1.5 kg/3 lb 5 oz baby back pork ribs
Mustard bourbon bbq sauce (*see* page 278)

Serves 4

1. Mix the ingredients for the dry rub in a medium bowl. Rub the mixture over both sides of the rib racks. Arrange the ribs on a large baking sheet. Cover and refrigerate overnight.

2. Preheat the barbecue to medium. Cut the rib racks into 4- to 6-rib sections. Arrange the ribs on the barbecue. Grill until the meat is tender, occasionally turning the ribs with tongs, about 40 minutes. Using tongs, transfer the ribs to a work surface.

3. Cut the rib sections between the bones into individual ribs. Arrange on a clean baking sheet. Brush the ribs with half of the Mustard bourbon bbq sauce. Place the remaining sauce in a small saucepan and reserve.

4. Return the ribs to the barbecue. Place the pan of reserved sauce at the edge of the barbecue to reheat. Grill the ribs until brown and crisp on the edges, brushing with more sauce and turning occasionally, about 10 minutes. Serve the ribs with warm sauce.

Spicy chicken satay skewers

600 g/1 lb 5 oz chicken
  breasts, cut into 2 cm/¾ in
  cubes or into strips
1 onion, finely chopped
1 stalk lemongrass, finely
  sliced
1 clove garlic, chopped
2.5 cm/1 in piece fresh ginger,
  finely chopped
1 tsp ground coriander
1 tsp ground cumin
½ tsp ground turmeric
½ tsp salt
1 tsp brown sugar
1 Tbsp soy sauce
3 Tbsp crunchy peanut butter
juice of 1 lime
1 Tbsp peanut or sunflower oil
Peanut sauce (*see* page 276),
  to serve

12 wooden or bamboo
  skewers, soaked

Makes 12

1. Thread about 5–6 cubes or 2 strips
of chicken on to each skewer and set aside
in a dish.

2. To make the satay mixture, put all the
remaining ingredients (except the Peanut
sauce) into a food processor and process
until everything is well blended and smooth.
Pour the satay mixture over the chicken,
using your hands to ensure it covers all the
surfaces, then cover and marinate in the
refrigerator for 1–2 hours or overnight.

3. When you are ready to cook, preheat the
barbecue or griddle pan to medium-hot.
Cook for 8–12 minutes, turning frequently,
or until cooked through and no pink juices
run when cut. Serve with Peanut sauce.

Italian-style sandwiches

2 chicken breasts

1 Tbsp olive oil

1 clove garlic, crushed

juice of 1 lemon

⅛ tsp salt

⅛ tsp pepper

1 red pepper, cored and cut into 8 wedges

olive oil for brushing

4 slices ciabatta or other crusty bread

Rosemary aïoli (*see* page 292)

1 handful rocket leaves

1 Tbsp capers

Serves 2

1. Combine chicken breasts in a bowl with olive oil, garlic, lemon juice, salt and pepper. Cover and leave to marinate for 20 minutes at room temperature, or up to 1 hour in the refrigerator.

2. Brush the red pepper wedges with olive oil. Preheat the barbecue or griddle pan to very hot. Grill the chicken for 4–6 minutes on each side, until cooked through. Meanwhile, grill the red peppers for 2–3 minutes on each side, until grill marks appear and skins are slightly charred. Transfer chicken and peppers to a chopping board and thinly slice.

3. To assemble the sandwiches, place 2 ciabatta slices on a chopping board. Spread Rosemary aïoli over them, top with chicken, red pepper, rocket and capers, then season with salt and pepper to taste. Cover with the remaining slices of bread and brush with oil. Grill the sandwiches on both sides, pressing gently with a spatula, until grill marks appear on the surface of the bread.

4. Transfer the sandwiches to serving plates, slice in half and serve immediately.

Veal & ham burgers with beetroot relish

4 large bread rolls

500 g/1lb minced veal

250 g/8 oz cooked ham, very finely chopped

2 eggs

1 tsp Tabasco sauce

1 Tbsp tomato sauce

60 g/2 oz onion, finely diced

1/2 tsp salt

dried breadcrumbs, if necessary

4 medium-size field mushrooms

3 oz shredded lettuce

For the beetroot relish:

220 g/7 oz beetroot, cooked, cooled and skins removed

2 salad onions, finely chopped

1 tsp anchovy sauce

1 Tbsp white wine vinegar

2 tsp truffle oil, or walnut oil

Serves 4

1. Cut bread rolls in half horizontally and pull out the soft centre of each half to make a well. Combine veal, ham, eggs, Tabasco, tomato sauce, onions, salt and the bread removed from the buns, broken into really small pieces. Using your hands, mix well. The bread you have used should be enough to bind the mixture, but if it is too moist, add enough dried breadcrumbs to take up any excess liquid. Shape into four patties – cover and refrigerate. Make relish by grating the beetroot roughly. Combine with salad onions, anchovy sauce, vinegar and oil and mix well.

2. Spray patties with oil and cook on the flat plate over medium heat for one minute. Spray again, turn and cook the second side for another minute. Spray mushrooms on the gill side (the brown underneath part) and cook on the open grill over high heat for two minutes on each side. Lift hamburger patties onto the open grill and cook over high heat for a further three minutes on each side, or until done to your liking. Spray insides of hamburger buns with oil and cook, cut-side-down, on the open grill for 30 seconds. Turn to cook for 30 seconds on the other side. Lift all ingredients from the barbecue and assemble by putting equal portions of lettuce in the base part of each bread roll. Add a cooked pattie and top with a mushroom. Spoon beetroot relish on top of the mushrooms and add the top part of the bread roll. Press down to compress the fillings and serve with your choice of salads.

Five-spice duck breasts

4 duck breasts, skin on
2 tsp Chinese 5-spice powder
4 heads pak choy
1 tsp olive oil

Serves 4

1. Pat the duck breasts dry using kitchen paper. With a sharp knife, cut diagonal, parallel slashes 2 cm/¾ in apart through the skin to make diamond shapes. Make sure that you do not cut right through and pierce the flesh. Rub ½ tsp of the Chinese 5-spice powder into the skin and flesh of the breast. Repeat with the remaining duck breasts. These can be left in the fridge for up to 12 hours.

2. To prepare the pak choy, bring a saucepan of water to the boil and plunge the pak choy in for about 1 minute, or until bright green in colour. Remove the heads immediately and cool under running cold water. Halve the pak choy lengthways and set aside.

3. Preheat the barbecue or griddle pan to medium-hot. Cook the duck skin-side down for about 5–6 minutes, until the skin is crispy. Turn and cook for a further 8–10 minutes, depending on how well done you like your duck. Remove from the barbecue or griddle pan, cover with foil and allow to rest for 5 minutes. While the duck rests, cook the pak choy on the barbecue or griddle pan for about 1 minute flat-side down and a further minute on the second side. Slice the duck just before serving and serve with one or two halves of pak choy.

Barbecued lamb with spiced couscous

For the lamb:

1 Tbsp crushed coriander seeds

freshly ground black pepper

12 halves (about 60 g/2 oz) semi-dried tomatoes, chopped

1 chargrilled yellow pepper, deseeded and chopped

120 g/4 oz black olives, drained

6 medium vine-ripened tomatoes, chopped

For the dressing:

3 Tbsp extra virgin olive oil

1 Tbsp white wine vinegar

1 clove garlic, peeled and crushed

¼ tsp salt and pepper to taste

1 Tbsp chopped Italian parsley

For the couscous:
See page 295

Serves 6

1. Rub lamb with crushed coriander seeds and 2 tablespoons of olive oil. Grind on plenty of black pepper. Cook over a high heat on a barbecue hot plate or over a barbecue grill rack (or roast in the oven). Transfer to a plate, sprinkle generously with salt and leave to rest for 5 minutes before slicing thinly across grain of meat.

2. Put semi-dried tomatoes in a bowl with yellow pepper and olives. Mix dressing ingredients together, except parsley, and toss through salad. Just before serving, stir through fresh tomatoes and parsley. Arrange couscous, salad and lamb on a large serving platter. Scatter over some more chopped mint and serve immediately.

NOTE
There are several cuts of lamb you can use in this recipe; here are some suggestions:

2 racks of lamb, trimmed, cut into mini racks of 3 cutlets each (cook for 10–12 minutes); 18 single cutlets (cook for 4–5 minutes); 3 lamb rumps about 180 g/6 oz each, trimmed (cook for 15–20 minutes); 8 lamb tenderloins, also known as lamb eye fillets, about 450 g/1 lb total (cook for 4–5 minutes). Allow meat to rest for a few minutes before serving and season with plenty of salt as soon as it comes off the barbecue.

Chicken fajitas

500 g/1 lb chicken breast meat

1 Tbsp corn oil

1 Tbsp Spanish sherry vinegar

1 Tbsp ground allspice

2 tsp dried oregano

2 Tbsp onion flakes

1 tsp salt

¼ tsp chilli powder (optional)

8 wheat flour tortillas

3 oz shredded lettuce

8 oz shaved carrot

2 medium-size salad tomatoes, cut into wedges

125 ml/4 fl oz sour cream

Serves 4

1. Cut chicken breast across the grain into strips 1 cm/½ in wide and place in a bowl. Combine the oil, sherry vinegar, allspice, oregano, onion flakes, salt and chilli powder, if using. Pour marinade over the chicken, stirring to coat the pieces thoroughly. Cover and refrigerate for at least two hours.

2. Spray the flat plate with oil and tip on the chicken strips – spread over the plate and cook by tossing and lifting the pieces, allowing them to brown. The chicken meat should cook in six minutes. Spray tortillas with oil and cook on the open grill for 30 seconds on each side. When tortillas are warm, remove from the open grill, lift the chicken onto a platter and return to the kitchen. Heap lettuce, carrot and tomatoes around the chicken.

3. Serve the chicken platter, tortillas and sour cream and let everybody assemble their own fajitas.

Yakitori

For the master sauce for all Yakitori:

125 ml/4 fl oz soy sauce

125 ml/4 fl oz mirin or dry sherry

1 Tbsp brown sugar

Chicken and spring onion yakitori:

4 skinless, boneless chicken thighs, cut into 18 x 3 cm/ 1¼ in cubes

5 spring onions, white and pale green parts only, cut into 12 x 3 cm/1¼ in lengths

Quail's egg yakitori:

18 quail's eggs, hard-boiled and shelled

6 x 15 cm/6 in wooden skewers, soaked for 1 hour

Each recipe makes 6 15 cm/6 in skewers

1. In a saucepan whisk together the soy sauce, mirin and sugar and bring the mixture to the boil over moderate heat. Simmer for 5 minutes, or until the sugar is dissolved, and the mixture begins to thicken. Set aside.

2. Thread the chicken and spring onion on to skewers, three pieces of chicken per skewer, or thread three quail eggs onto each skewer.

3. Preheat the barbecue or griddle pan to hot. Brush the skewers with master sauce. Grill the chicken skewers for 2–3 minutes on each side, until cooked through. The quail eggs only need 1 minute per side. Baste the skewers liberally with the master sauce while grilling. Serve immediately with extra sauce for dipping.

Honey soy butterflied char-roasted chicken

2 corn-fed chickens

3 cloves garlic, peeled and grated

4 Tbsp runny honey

3 Tbsp Dijon mustard

2 Tbsp dark soy sauce

1 Tbsp dry sherry

1 Tbsp lemon juice

olive oil

Serves 8-10

1. Pat dry the chickens with absorbent kitchen paper. Using a pair of kitchen scissors, cut along each side of the backbone. Lift out and discard (backbones can be frozen and used for chicken stock). Turn the chickens skin-side up and press down to flatten them.

2. Combine the garlic, honey, mustard, soy sauce, sherry and lemon juice. Using a sharp knife, make deep slash marks through the skin of the drumsticks and thighs. Massage the marinade well into the surface area of both chickens. Cover and refrigerate for 1 hour.

3. Preheat the oven to 180 °C/350 °F (gas 4). Place the chickens in a roasting pan and roast for 30 minutes. Remove the chickens from the oven and finish cooking them, covered, over medium heat on a barbecue grill for a further 20-30 minutes, basting them from time to time with the remaining marinade and a little olive oil until they are cooked through. Place the chickens on a serving platter and spoon over the remaining marinade and juices.

Lamb cutlets with soy and honey aubergine

4 baby aubergines, about 90 g/2 oz each

2 Tbsp dark soy sauce

2 Tbsp light olive oil

1 Tbsp honey

½ tsp freshly ground black pepper

12 trimmed lamb cutlets, each 2 cm/¾ in thick

1 tsp salt

Serves 4

1. Top and tail aubergine and slice in half lengthwise. Score the flesh by making diagonal cuts to form diamond shapes, being careful not to cut through the skin. Mix the soy, oil, honey and pepper.

2. Brush soy mixture on the cut side of the aubergine halves, ensuring that some penetrates down into the scored flesh. Spray the flat plate with oil and cook aubergine halves, cut-side-down, for two minutes. Turn and cook for a further one minute. At the same time, cook cutlets on the open grill for two minutes on each side, sprinkling with salt when you turn them.

3. Place two aubergine halves, cut-side-up, on each plate. Stack three lamb cutlets adjacent to the aubergine and serve with salads of your choice.

Chargrilled duck breasts and curried chickpeas

4 x 250 g/8 oz Muscovy duck
   breasts

Curried chickpeas
   (*see* page 294)

2 Tbsp rice vinegar

½ Tbsp cooking salt

1 Tbsp Sumac

Serves 4

1. Slash the skin side of the breasts to allow the fat to escape during cooking. Have the Curried chickpeas ready for reheating.

2. Rub the vinegar into the skin side of the duck breasts. Lay them over the high-heat part of the open slats, skin sides down, and leave there for 1–2 minutes. Watch the breasts carefully as flames can scorch the skin, rather than brown it. Sprinkle the flesh side of the breasts with a little salt and half the Sumac and turn over. Sprinkle the skin sides with the remaining salt and Sumac and leave to cook for 1 minute. Turn the breasts back onto their skin sides and move to a part of the open slats where the temperature is medium. Leave to cook a further 2–3 minutes. Turn breasts over and cook on the flesh side until done, 5–7 minutes. By now, the skin should be crispy and browned. Remove from the barbecue when done and let rest for at least 10 minutes before slicing.

3. Either heat the Curried chickpeas in the microwave or in a saucepan on the stove top. Cut the duck breasts on the diagonal. Place the chickpeas in the centre of a serving plate or bowl, top with the slices of duck and serve.

Orange-scented meatloaf

500 g/1 lb lean minced beef

1 cup dried breadcrumbs

1 small onion, finely chopped

1 Tbsp minced fresh ginger

1 Tbsp chopped chervil, or oregano

1 tsp salt

juice and finely grated rind of 1 orange

1 large egg, beaten

2 Tbsp seeded Dijon mustard

Homemade barbecue sauce (*see* recipe page 273), to serve

Serves 4

1. Combine all ingredients and, using your hands or a fork, mix thoroughly. Take a large sheet of thick foil and spray with olive oil. Tip the mixture onto the foil and shape into a large sausage about 23 cm/9 in long and 6 cm/2½ in in diameter. Wrap the foil around to hold the meat in place and twist the ends to seal. Refrigerate for at least one hour.

2. Cook the loaf on the flat plate for 40 minutes, turning every 10 minutes to ensure even cooking. Remove from barbecue and leave to rest for 10 minutes before peeling away the foil.

3. Slice and serve with a salad and homemade barbecue sauce.

Spicy lamb on sticks with yoghurt sauce

650 g/1 lb 4 oz prime minced lamb (or beef)

1 medium onion, peeled and finely chopped

1 clove garlic, peeled and crushed

1 tsp finely grated fresh ginger

1 1/2 tsp salt

1 tsp garam masala

2 Tbsp finely chopped coriander

1 egg

60 ml/2 fl oz water

2 Tbsp besan (chick pea flour)

fluffy steamed rice for serving (optional)

For the yoghurt sauce:

8 fl oz plain unsweetened yoghurt

pinch of salt

2 Tbsp chopped mint

1 hot green chilli, deseeded and finely chopped

Serves 3–4 (Makes about 12 meatballs)

1. Put minced meat in a large bowl and add onion, garlic, ginger, salt, garam masala and coriander. Beat egg and water together, add to minced meat mixture, then sprinkle on chick pea flour. Knead mixture together thoroughly with your hands.

2. Shape meat into small 'sausage' shapes, transferring them to a plate as they are prepared. Cover and chill meatballs for 1–2 hours before cooking them.

3. In a bowl mix ingredients for Yoghurt Sauce. Cover and set aside.

4. Put two meatballs on each skewer. The best skewers are the flatter kind; the meat flops around on smooth, round metal skewers (but if preferred you can forgo skewers and cook meatballs individually). Carefully transfer skewers to a lightly oiled barbecue hot plate and cook over a medium–high heat until cooked through (you'll need to cut one open to check). Finish cooking them over a hot barbecue grill rack. Serve hot with Yoghurt Sauce and plenty of fluffy steamed rice.

Chicken skewers on watermelon and feta salad

For the chicken skewers:

2 yellow peppers

245 g/8½ oz jar pimiento-stuffed green olives (or queen olives, which are even better), drained

4 Tbsp olive oil

1 lemon

1 Tbsp honey

2 Tbsp finely chopped mint, plus extra sprigs for garnishing

salt and freshly ground black pepper

750 g/1 lb 6 oz skinned and boned chicken breasts, cut into small pieces

For the salad:
See page 290

Serves 6 (makes approx 24 skewers)

1. Core and deseed peppers and cut them into smallish chunks. Put in a bowl with olives and mix in 1 tablespoon of olive oil. Set aside for 15 minutes.

2. Peel off lemon rind in long thin strips and juice the lemon. Put rind in a bowl with strained lemon juice and honey, the rest of the oil, mint, ¼ teaspoon of salt and pepper. Mix well, then add chicken pieces, stirring well to coat. Thread chicken onto bamboo skewers alternating with chunks of yellow pepper and olives.

3. Cook over a medium heat on a barbecue hot plate until chicken is lightly browned and cooked through; do not have the heat too high or the outside of chicken will brown before the inside cooks properly. Drizzle with marinade during cooking, but take care that lemon rind does not burn. To avoid this happening, scrape pieces of lemon rind onto hot plate and cook separately until golden, then put on top of the skewers once they are cooked (they have a delicious intense lemony flavour).

4. Have ready a salad (*see* page 290). Put the hot chicken kebabs on top and garnish with mint sprigs. Serve immediately.

Devilled chicken wings

60 ml/2 fl oz extra virgin
   olive oil

1 tsp paprika

1 tsp ground cumin

finely grated zest of 1 lemon

freshly ground black pepper
   to taste

1 kg/2 lb 2 oz chicken wings,
   halved

salt

lime wedges for serving

Serves 4

1. In a shallow dish mix oil, paprika, cumin, lemon zest and a good grinding of black pepper. Add chicken wings and turn to coat in dressing. Cover and marinate for at least 1 hour, but up to 24 hours, refrigerated, turning occasionally.

2. Gently turn chicken wings in dressing, adding 1/2 teaspoon of salt. Cook over a low to medium heat on an oiled barbecue hot plate for about 45 minutes or until cooked through and well coloured; baste with marinade juices from time to time. Alternatively, cook in an oven preheated to 180 °C/350 °F (gas 4) for about 25 minutes or until golden and cooked through.

3. Transfer chicken wings to a platter, sprinkle with salt and squeeze over lime wedges. Serve hottish or at room temperature as a nibble or as part of a barbecue meal.

Loin of lamb with plum tomatoes and butternut squash

500 g/1 lb boneless loin of lamb
(ask your butcher to cut it crosswise
into 4 steaks)

2 Tbsp extra virgin olive oil

2 parsnips, each about 220 g/7 oz

2 Roma (plum) tomatoes, cut in half
lengthwise

¼ tsp salt

1 butternut squash, about 750 g/1 lb 6 oz

balsamic vinegar

Serves 4

1. Trim lamb steaks, place in a bowl and pour olive oil over to coat. Peel parsnips and cut off any of the fibrous end pieces. Cut each into four wedges and remove the woody core. Sprinkle the cut side of the tomatoes with salt. Cut the squash in half lengthwise. Cover one half with plastic wrap and refrigerate for another use. Cook remaining half, with seeds still in, in the microwave on high for seven minutes.

2. Spray cut side of squash with oil and cook on the open grill over high heat for five minutes. Turn over and leave to cook for 10 minutes. Scoop out the seeds at this stage with a spoon taking care as the squash will be hot. Spray parsnips with oil and cook on the open grill over high heat for four minutes.

3. Lift parsnip onto the flat plate and cook over medium heat for a further four minutes, turning regularly. Turn over the squash again and leave to cook for 10 minutes. Spray cut side of tomato halves with oil and cook, cut-side-down, on the flat plate for two minutes. Turn and cook for two minutes more. Cook oiled lamb steaks on the flat plate over medium heat for four minutes on each side. Rest for four minutes before slicing and serving.

4. Collect all the barbecued ingredients onto a large platter and return to the kitchen. Slice squash into eight even portions and place two pieces in the centre of each plate. Sit two pieces of parsnip on top of the squash and top with a half tomato, cut-side-up. Cut lamb on the diagonal and place two pieces on each plate, standing them against the stacked vegetables. Sprinkle with a little balsamic vinegar and serve immediately.

Pork fillet with courgette and spaghetti

410 g/13 oz pork fillet, trimmed

315 g/10 oz medium dried spaghetti

90 g/3 oz courgette, finely sliced into rounds

90 g/3 oz white onion, sliced in rings

2 cloves garlic, peeled and crushed

150 ml/5 fl oz white wine

1 Tbsp freshly chopped Italian parsley

1 tsp freshly chopped marjoram

½ tsp salt

½ tsp cracked black pepper

1 Tbsp extra virgin olive oil

Serves 4

1. Slice pork fillet into rounds 2 cm/¾ in thick and flatten with your hand to about half the thickness.

2. Bring a large pot of salted water to the boil and drop in the spaghetti. To cook al dente takes about eight to nine minutes, but in this case, the pasta must not be overcooked. When just done, strain and run under warm water. If you use it straight away there is no need to rub oil through the spaghetti.

3. Spray pork fillet pieces with oil and cook on the flat plate for two minutes on each side. At the same time, add courgette, onion and garlic to another part of the oiled plate. Cook vegetables, moving them around, for three minutes.

4. When pork is cooked combine it with the vegetables and add the spaghetti. Pour over half the wine and, using two spatulas, lift and combine spaghetti with meat and vegetable mixture. Cook like this for a further three minutes and add remaining wine.

5. Sprinkle with parsley, marjoram, salt and pepper, lifting and tossing to spread the flavours through the spaghetti. Make sure you scrape up the tasty caramelized pieces while turning the vegetables and spaghetti.

6. Lift the cooked ingredients into a big bowl, drizzle with olive oil and serve with a salad of your choice and crusty bread.

Prosciutto-wrapped lamb cutlets

16 French lamb cutlets

2 Tbsp Dijon mustard

16 thin slices prosciutto

16 sprigs rosemary

Serves 4

1. Lay the cutlets flat on a chopping board and spread with a little mustard. Wrap each cutlet in a slice of prosciutto and insert a sprig of rosemary.

2. Grill the cutlets on a hot barbecue grill for approximately 3 minutes on each side or until the prosciutto is crisp and the lamb medium-rare.

Sweet barbecue ribs

3 small pork racks, cut into
  single ribs

1 Tbsp olive oil

4 cloves garlic, peeled and
  crushed

120 g/4 oz tomato purée

120 ml/4 fl oz pineapple juice

120 ml/4 fl oz balsamic vinegar

60 ml/2 fl oz soy sauce

120 ml/6 fl oz honey

sea salt and freshly ground
  black pepper

Serves 6

1. Place the ribs in a shallow pan. Combine the remaining ingredients and pour over the ribs to coat. Transfer the pan to the fridge and marinate for 2 hours.

2. Remove the ribs from the marinade, brushing off any excess. Retain the marinade.

3. Barbeque the ribs over medium heat for 20-30 minutes or until well-browned, cooked and caramelized on the outside. Place the remaining marinade in a saucepan and reduce by half over a low heat. When the ribs are done place on a serving plate and pour over the reduced marinade. Serve immediately.

Fish and seafood

Bream fillets with mangetout and garlic potato bake

4 x 180 g/6 oz bream fillets

oil spray

sea salt

300 g/10 oz mangetout, trimmed

4 lemon cheeks

garlic potato bake (see below)

For the garlic potato bake:

30 g/1 oz butter

1 Tbsp olive oil

3 leeks, white only, cleaned and sliced thinly

4 cloves garlic, chopped

300 ml/10 fl oz pouring cream

4 large potatoes, peeled and sliced thinly

salt and pepper to taste

3 Tbsp chopped parsley

Serves 4

1. To make the potato bake, pan fry leeks in foaming butter and oil until soft. Add garlic, stir, add cream and reduce until thick. Place potatoes in a bowl and pour over creamed leek, season with salt and pepper, parsley and mix gently.

2. Line a heavy oven dish or ovenproof frying pan with baking paper and press in potatoes. Bake in a moderate oven for about 1 hour. When cooked, allow to cool slightly before turning out and slicing into wedges. This can be made in advance.

3. Trim the fish if necessary. Spray the skin side with oil and sprinkle on a little sea salt. Put fish, skin side down, onto a hot flat plate and press down with a spatula, which prevents the fillet from curling. Repeat with all the fillets, spray the flesh side with oil and turn after 1–2 minutes. The skin can go quite crispy and the cooking time will depend on the thickness of the fillets.

4. Drop the mangetout into boiling salted water and cook for 1–2 minutes depending on their size. Thinner ones take much less time to cook through. Strain and serve immediately.

5. Place a wedge of the potato bake with the point in the centre of each plate. Put a pile of mangetout around that point and place a piece of fish, skin side up, on the mangetout, with the lemon to one side.

Spanish mackerel kebabs with mango and lychee salsa

600 g/1 lb 2 oz Spanish mackerel fillets

1 Tbsp sesame seeds

½ Tbsp sesame oil

1 Tbsp rice oil

2 fl oz/60 ml soy sauce

250 g/8 oz mango flesh, diced

125 g/4 oz lychees, deseeded and diced

125 g/4 oz spring onions, finely diced

2 fl oz/60 ml lime juice

8 coriander leaves, roughly chopped

1 tsp fish sauce

1 large green fruity chilli, minced

coriander leaves for decoration

Serves 4

1. Cut the mackerel into even sized pieces. Thread equal quantities onto oiled stainless skewers. Refrigerate until ready for use.

2. Make the sesame baste by pounding the seeds in a mortar and pestle and then, when crushed, adding the oils and soy sauce – mix well and set to one side.

3. Make the salsa by combining the mango, lychees, green spring onion, lime juice, roughly chopped coriander leaves, fish sauce and chilli – gently toss. Refrigerate until ready for use.

4. Brush the fish kebabs with the sesame baste and place onto a medium–hot flat plate. Turn regularly and carefully and baste as you go.

5. Spoon salsa into the middle of individual plates, top with kebabs and decorate with plenty of coriander leaves.

Chived eggs with smoked salmon and brioche

8 free-range eggs

3 Tbsp chopped chives

30 g/1 oz butter, melted and returned to room temperature

¼ tsp freshly ground black pepper

4–8 slices brioche

8 slices smoked salmon

Serves 4

1. Take two bowls and beat four eggs well in each bowl. Stir half the chives, butter and black pepper into each batch.

2. Spray brioche lightly with oil and toast on both sides on the open grill. Place slice(s) on four individual plates and start cooking the eggs.

3. Oil the flat plate liberally and pour one batch of eggs on – use a spatula to keep them from running all over the plate. This is like making eggs in a frying pan rather than a saucepan – you must keep the egg mixture constantly moving around a concentrated area on the barbecue plate. Each batch will take 45 to 50 seconds to cook and must retain a gloss on the top.

4. Divide the first batch of scrambled eggs between two of the plates, placing on top of the brioche. Cook the second batch in the same way, and divide between the remaining two plates.

5. Top scrambled eggs with the salmon slices and serve immediately.

Tuna stuffed with sesame greens

2 thick tuna steaks about
200 g/7 oz each and at least
3 cm/1¼ in thick

2 spring onions, white parts
only, finely chopped

1 tsp finely chopped fresh
ginger

½ tsp finely chopped garlic

½ tsp sesame seeds

2 tsp soy sauce

1 tsp sesame oil plus extra to
baste

2 tsp vegetable oil

50 g/2 oz watercress or other
small yet sturdy greens

Serves 2

1. Preheat the barbecue or griddle pan to very hot.

2. Place the tuna steaks on a chopping board. Place one hand firmly on the tuna. With a small, sharp knife, make a small incision into the steak, creating a pocket.

3. Combine the spring onions, ginger, garlic, sesame seeds, soy sauce, sesame oil and vegetable oil in a small bowl. Toss with the watercress.

4. Carefully stuff the tossed watercress into each tuna steak, pushing well inside the steaks. Reserve any extra watercress for garnish. Brush the steaks generously with sesame oil and place on the grill. Sear on both sides until browned, about 30 seconds on each side. Reduce the heat (or, if using charcoal, move to an area of the grill where there are no coals underneath) and allow the steaks to cook for 3–4 minutes on each side for medium steaks.

5. Serve the tuna steaks cut in half to expose the watercress inside. Garnish with any remaining tossed watercress.

Grilled crayfish with lemon butter

For the lemon butter:

150 g/5 oz butter, softened

Finely grated rind of 2 lemons

Salt and freshly ground black pepper

2 large crayfish or lobster, live if possible

1 Tbsp olive oil

4 lemons, halved

1 handful basil

Serves 2–4

1. Prepare the lemon butter well in advance. Put the butter, lemon rind, salt and pepper in a food processor and pulse until well blended. Lay out a large piece of foil, about 25 cm/10 in square, on a flat surface, put the butter in the centre and shape into a log. Roll up the foil, shaping the butter into an even log shape, and twist the ends to secure it. Refrigerate the butter for at least 4 hours or, if time is limited, freeze for about 45 minutes. If cutting the butter from frozen make sure you warm the knife slightly first. Remove the butter from the fridge just before serving to soften slightly.

2. Kill and cut your crayfish in half (see page 21).

3. Preheat the barbecue to medium. Lightly oil the crayfish on the flesh side. Place the crayfish flesh-side down on the hot rack. Grill for 5 minutes. Turn the crayfish over, rub a slice of lemon butter over the surface and cook for a further 8–10 minutes, moving them around the rack occasionally. For the last 2–3 minutes, place the lemon halves flat-side down on the grill and cook. Serve with grilled lemon halves, another slice of lemon butter and freshly torn basil leaves.

Cuttlefish with spicy Italian sausage and pine nut salad

500 g/1 lb cuttlefish, body only and
   with cuttlebone removed

2 Tbsp extra virgin olive oil

250 g/8 oz spicy Italian sausage,
   around 3 cm/1¼ in in diameter

60 g/2 oz pine nuts, toasted

mesclun salad mix

20 grape tomatoes, halved

2 Tbsp zest of lemon, finely grated

60 ml/2 fl oz lemon juice

2 Tbsp Italian parsley, finely chopped

sea salt, to taste

60 ml/2 fl oz olive oil

Serves 4

1. Cut the cuttlefish open to form one large flat piece and trim. With a very sharp knife, score the flesh into diamond shapes. Cut into bite-sized pieces, place in a bowl and pour over the 2 tablespoons of virgin olive oil. Toss the cuttlefish in the oil and allow to rest for 15 minutes. If you wish to use later, refrigerate it. Cut the sausage into rounds approximately 1 cm/½ in thick. Place the nuts, mesclun and tomato halves in a salad bowl and refrigerate.

2. Put the cuttlefish on the flat plate with the scored side down. Toss once the scored side is lightly browned – cuttlefish cooks quickly and if overcooked becomes tough. Remove cuttlefish from the barbecue and put in a bowl. Add the lemon zest, lemon juice, parsley and sea salt; toss to coat and allow to cool. Put the sausage slices on the open slats to crisp and turn brown. Remove from the barbecue when done, approximately 1–2 minutes on each cut side.

3. Pour the 60 ml/2 fl oz of olive oil over the salad mix and toss. Divide the sausage slices among individual plates, place some salad on top and arrange the pieces of the cuttlefish on top and around the salad.

Whole trout stuffed with lemon and dill

1 small trout, about 500 g/1 lb,
   gutted
2–3 sprigs dill
1 tsp cold butter, cut in half
1 slice lemon, cut into 4 pieces
salt and pepper, to taste
vegetable oil, for brushing

Serves 1

1. Preheat the barbecue to medium.

2. Open the cavity of the fish and place dill,
butter and pieces of lemon inside. Season.

3. Take a sheet of foil one and a half times
the length of the fish and brush it lightly with
vegetable oil. Place the trout in the centre
of the foil, bring the long edges together
and loosely fold. Scrunch the ends to form
a loose yet airtight rectangular package.
Place the package on the barbecue and
cover. Grill for about 8 minutes. To check if
the fish is ready, remove the package from
the barbecue, open it and insert a wooden
skewer into the thickest part of the fish. If the
fish is ready the skewer should glide in easily.
If you are unsure, peel back a small piece of
skin and look closely at the flesh – if it is still
transparent close the package and grill for
another 1–2 minutes. When the trout is
cooked, unwrap the package and carefully
transfer the fish to a plate. Pour butter juices
from the package over the fish and serve.

Barbecued prawns with glass noodle salad

20 green king prawns, body peeled and heads and tails left on

2 Tbsp pineapple juice, from fresh pineapple

2 Tbsp peanut or vegetable oil

1 Tbsp fish sauce

1 clove garlic, crushed

1 Tbsp green ginger, minced

1 tsp white sugar

Glass noodle salad (*see* recipe page 289)

Serves 4

1. Devein the prawns (optional). Squeeze the flesh of a peeled and chopped pineapple to extract the juice. Mix all the remaining ingredients together – except for the Glass noodle salad – and add the prawns. Coat prawns well and allow to marinate for 20 minutes. Make the Glass noodle salad.

2. Barbecue the prawns on the open slats for approximately 1–2 minutes each side, depending on their size.

3. Have the salad arranged on a large platter and top with the prawns. Serve immediately.

Almond and parsley-crusted snapper fillets

4 x 180 g snapper fillets

30 g/1 oz flat leaf parsley leaves, finely chopped

60 g/2 oz green spring onions, finely chopped

60 g/2 oz almonds, skin on and finely chopped

1 clove garlic, minced

1 Tbsp capers, rinsed

30 g/1 oz breadcrumbs, fresh

1 egg white

vegetable oil spray

baking paper

4 lemon wedges

Serves 4

1. Trim the fish fillets if necessary and refrigerate until ready to cook.

2. Mix the parsley, spring onions, almonds, garlic, capers and breadcrumbs. Whisk the egg white with a fork and tip half into the crust mixture and tumble to combine well.

3. Pat the fish dry with paper towelling and brush with remaining half egg white. Spoon and pat a layer of the parsley mix onto each fish fillet. Spray a suitably sized flat baking tray with oil, line with baking paper and spray the paper with oil. Carefully lift the snapper fillets onto the baking tray.

4. Put a cake cooling rack or similar onto the hot flat plate and sit the fish on that. Cook on a moderately hot barbecue with the lid down for 6–8 minutes – time depends on the thickness of the fish fillet.

5. Remove and serve with a lemon wedge to one side and a good big bowl of a mixed green leaf salad.

Scallops with white bean purée and pannini bruschetta

12 large sea scallops

For the white bean purée:
200 g/7 oz tinned cannellini beans, drained
1 clove garlic
sea salt and cayenne pepper, to taste
60 ml/2 fl oz olive oil

For the pannini bruschetta:
8 slices pannini
oil spray
1 very ripe red tomato, halved
ground black pepper
extra virgin olive oil
fresh basil leaves

Serves 4

1. Trim the scallops of the vein that runs around the side of each one. Refrigerate until ready for use. Cover the beans with water. Add the garlic, salt and cayenne, and simmer for 15 minutes. Drain and tip into a food processor bowl. Start processing, pouring the oil in slowly so it is incorporated into a smooth paste.

2. Remove bean purée from the bowl and keep warm. Refrigerate the bean purée if not using immediately.

3. Spray the pannini with oil and place on open slats. Turn to check it is lightly brown; note that pannini browns quickly. When browned on both sides, lift from the barbecue and rub pannini with the cut part of the tomato halves, squeezing the flesh so that some adheres to the pannini. Spray the scallops with oil and flash-cook them on the flat plate. Scallops cook extremely quickly, so turn them after 30 seconds to check they are sealed and browned. Remove immediately when cooked.

4. If you have refrigerated the bean purée, reheat it in a microwave. Divide the warm bean purée among the four plates, placing it in the centre of each plate. Place three scallops on top, sprinkle over a little ground black pepper, drizzle with a little extra virgin olive oil and decorate with fresh basil leaves. Serve the bruschetta in a bread basket.

Chef Jon's dry cured salt-sugar salmon

100 g/3½ oz coarse sea salt
100 g/3½ oz caster sugar
grated rind of 1 lemon
1 Tbsp fennel seeds (optional)
4 salmon fillets, about
  120 g/4 oz each, skin on
vegetable oil, for grilling

Serves 4

1. Combine the salt, sugar, lemon rind and fennel seeds in a shallow baking dish. Bury the fillets in the mixture. Cover with plastic food wrap and refrigerate for 2–3 hours.

2. Remove the fish from the refrigerator 20 minutes before grilling. Heat a griddle pan or barbecue to very hot. Brush the grill with oil. Lift the fillets from the sugar and salt mixture and rinse under running water. The surface of the fish will be deep in colour, and almost caramelized in texture. Grill, skin-side down, for 4–5 minutes, until the skin is charred and the fish is uniform in colour. Lift from the grill and serve.

Blackened halibut

For the rub:

1 tsp salt

1 tsp dried thyme

½ tsp dried oregano

½ tsp cayenne pepper

¼ tsp hot paprika

½ tsp freshly ground black
  pepper

½ tsp fennel seeds, toasted
  and roughly chopped

salt and pepper, to taste

4 halibut fillets,
  200 g/7 oz each

olive oil, for brushing

1 lime, quartered

Serves 4

1. Combine the ingredients for the rub in a small bowl. Place the halibut fillets in a shallow baking dish and brush with oil. Pat the rub all over the fish. Season with more salt and pepper. Cover and chill for up to 1 hour, in the refrigerator.

2. Preheat the barbecue or griddle pan to hot. Brush the grill bars well with oil. Grill the fillets for 2–2½ minutes on each side, until charred and just cooked through. Serve immediately with a squeeze of lime.

Barbecued tuna steak 'niçoise'

60 ml/2 fl oz extra virgin
  olive oil

30 ml/1 fl oz wine vinegar

155 g/5 oz green beans,
  whole, topped, tailed
  and blanched

155 g/5 oz Desiree potatoes,
  sliced 2 cm/¾ in thick and
  par-boiled for 5 minutes

4 x 110 g/4 oz tuna steaks,
  about 2 cm/¾ in thick

3 Roma (plum) tomatoes,
  trimmed at either end and
  cut into wedges

2 hard-boiled eggs, peeled
  and quartered

20 black olives

4–8 anchovy fillets

cracked black pepper
  (optional)

Serves 4

1. Mix olive oil and vinegar together.

2. Lightly spray beans with oil and toss on the flat plate. Move these around quickly for one minute and don't let them brown. Lift onto a platter. Spray potato slices with oil and cook on each side for one minute, or until done. Lift and place on the beans. Spray tuna with oil and cook on the flat plate for one minute on each side.

3. Meanwhile, spread tomatoes, hard-boiled eggs and black olives over the top of the potatoes and beans. Arrange anchovy fillets on the vegetables. Remove tuna from barbecue and arrange on top. Spoon oil and vinegar dressing over the tuna and sprinkle with cracked black pepper, if desired.

Whole snapper with lentil and Spanish onion salad

4 snapper, each 500 g/17½ oz

1 small lemon, cut into quarters

8 spring onions, white parts only

90 g/3 oz butter, melted

1 tsp sea salt

½ tsp freshly ground black pepper

4 sheets of aluminium foil, sprayed with oil

For the lentil and Spanish onion salad:
See page 291

Serves 4–6

1. Rinse fish cavities with cold water and dry with paper towel. Cut two deep diagonal slashes into each side of each fish. Lay one fish on each piece of oiled foil and stuff each gut cavity with a lemon quarter and two green onions. (You may have to cut the green onions to fit in the cavity.) Spoon over the melted butter and sprinkle with salt and pepper. Wrap fish in the foil, making sure that the foil is tight around the fish so that the juices can't escape during cooking. Refrigerate parcels for 30 minutes.

2. Place fish parcels on the flat plate and cook for eight minutes on each side. Lift fish parcels onto individual plates and allow each person to open the foil to reveal the beautifully cooked fish. The wonderful aroma of lemon and green onion escapes as the parcels are opened. Serve the lentil salad in the centre of the table with a mixed leaf salad.

Prawn and chorizo skewers

12 large prawns

1 Tbsp harissa paste (optional)

2 chorizo sausages,
about 150 g/6 oz each

12 fresh bay leaves

1 Tbsp olive oil

12 short skewers, soaked if
wood or bamboo

Makes 12

1. Peel and devein the prawns, leaving the small tail ends still attached. Rub over the harissa paste evenly and set aside. Slice the chorizo into 1½ cm/½ in thick slices. Place 1 chorizo slice into the crook of each prawn and thread onto a skewer. Add a bay leaf to each skewer and refrigerate until ready to cook.

2. Preheat the barbecue or griddle pan to medium-hot. Brush the skewers with a little olive oil and cook for 5–6 minutes, turning once, or until the prawns are translucent and the chorizo cooked through. Serve immediately.

Whole sardines with capers and pinenuts

12 fresh sardines, cleaned (gut removed)

60 g/2 oz capers, drained and washed

45 g/1½ oz pinenuts

¼ tsp ground cumin

lemon wedges or cheeks, to serve (optional)

Serves 4

1. Rinse sardines and pat dry. Combine capers and pinenuts.

2. Spray the flat plate with oil and cook sardines for one-and-a-half minutes. Spray sardines with oil and, using a long spatula, gently turn them over. Cook for a further one-and-a-half minutes.

3. Meanwhile, pour the capers and pinenuts onto the flat plate. Cook for three minutes, tossing and moving them about but keeping them in a concentrated area. The pinenuts will be lightly browned and the capers warmed through. Lift capers and pinenuts from the barbecue, place at one end of a platter and sprinkle with cumin. Remove sardines from the barbecue and place on the same platter.

4. The sardines can be eaten whole, bones and all, with the capers and pinenuts as a tasty addition. Serve with lemon wedges or cheeks, if desired.

Skewered tikka-infused snapper with cucumber and mint dip

600 g snapper fillets, cut into bite-sized pieces

4–8 stainless steel skewers

240 ml/8 fl oz natural yoghurt

1 Tbsp cider vinegar

2 Tbsp tikka paste

1 Tbsp mint

4–8 lime cheeks

For the cucumber and mint dip:

240 ml/8 fl oz natural yoghurt

40 g/1½ oz cucumber flesh, finely diced

2 Tbsp mint, finely shredded

Serves 4

1. Thread equal numbers of snapper pieces onto the skewers. Mix the yoghurt, vinegar, tikka paste and mint together.

2. On a large, flat glass dish, spoon the tikka mixture over the fish skewers and let them sit in the marinade for at least 30 minutes. Turn every 10 minutes or spoon the marinade over them.

3. Cook on a medium–hot flat plates until done. Turn regularly and brush with the tikka mixture as you go. These will take around 10 minutes to cook and they go quite crusty as they do.

4. Serve on a platter, with the lime cheeks, in the middle of the table with a bowl of the dipping sauce beside the fish. A good green salad and some heated pita bread or naan completes this dish.

5. To make the dip, mix well at least 4 hours before use, and refrigerate.

Veggie

Aubergines with pomegranate

4 baby aubergines about
    100 g/3½ oz each or
    1 large aubergine

olive oil, for brushing

salt and pepper, to taste

100 g/3½ oz baby spinach

50 g/2 oz feta cheese
    (optional)

1 Tbsp pine nuts, toasted

2 Tbsp finely chopped mint

1 pomegranate, seeds
    removed and set aside,
    flesh discarded

For the dressing:
2 heaped Tbsp plain yoghurt

½ tsp ground cumin

1 Tbsp pomegranate molasses

½ tsp caster sugar

1 tsp lemon juice

Serves 4

1. Heat the barbecue or griddle pan to medium-hot.

2. Slice the aubergines into 1 cm/½ in thick circles and brush with olive oil. Grill until the surface is crisp, the centres are soft and grill marks appear on the surface. Transfer to a plate and sprinkle with salt and pepper. Leave to cool.

3. Arrange the spinach on a platter and top with aubergine, feta (if using), pine nuts, mint and pomegranate seeds.

4. In a small bowl, whisk the dressing ingredients together and drizzle over the salad.

Smoky Portobello mushroom burger

4 large Portobello mushrooms, stems removed

Handful of wood chips, soaked for 1 hour (optional)

4 hamburger buns, sliced in half

For the marinade:
125 ml/4 fl oz olive oil

75 ml/2½ fl oz red wine vinegar

2 Tbsp Dijon mustard

2 cloves garlic, thinly sliced

1 Tbsp fresh thyme

1 Tbsp chopped basil

½ tsp sea salt

⅛ tsp pepper

Suggested toppings:
Mayonnaise, Dijon mustard, mature Cheddar cheese slices, lettuce leaves, sliced tomatoes, thinly sliced red onion

Serves 4

1. Place the mushrooms in a shallow baking dish. In a small bowl, whisk the marinade ingredients together and drizzle over the mushrooms, turning to coat. Cover and refrigerate for at least 30 minutes or up to 3 hours.

2. Preheat the barbecue or griddle pan to medium-high heat. Grill the mushrooms for 3–4 minutes on each side, until browned and very tender. Toast the buns on the bars until lightly toasted.

3. Place the mushrooms on the bottom half of the buns. Top with your chosen toppings, and cover with the top half of the buns. Serve immediately.

Vegetable and taleggio tortilla toasties

1 large aubergine

2 courgettes

2 red or yellow peppers

2 Tbsp olive oil

salt and freshly ground black pepper

8 flour tortillas

1 Tbsp capers, rinsed

1 handful basil

250 g/8 oz taleggio cheese

Serves 4

1. Preheat the griddle pan or barbecue grill plate to very hot. Slice the aubergines and courgettes into 3–5 mm/⅛–¼ in thick slices. Quarter and deseed the peppers. Brush the vegetables with little oil and grill for 2–3 minutes on each side or until soft, cooked and browned. When all the vegetables are cooked, set aside to cool then cut up into small cubes, about 1–2 cm/½–¾ in square. Season generously with salt and pepper.

2. Preheat the barbecue hot plate or griddle pan to medium. Lay out a tortilla on a flat surface and evenly spread over a quarter of the vegetable mixture and capers. Tear over a few basil leaves and top with a quarter of the cheese, cut into small cubes. Place a second tortilla on top then transfer to the pan or barbecue. Cook for 2–3 minutes on each side or until golden brown and the cheese is starting to ooze. Repeat until all four are cooked, keeping them warm as you go under a clean tea towel or in a very low oven. Cut up into wedges and serve with your favourite relish, Sweet Thai chilli sauce (*see page 274*) or tomato sauce.

Grilled courgette and mint salad

6 courgettes, about
 1 kg/2 lb 4 oz in total, sliced
 lengthways into
 1–2 mm/$\frac{1}{16}$ in thick slices

2 Tbsp extra virgin olive oil

For the dressing:

juice of 1 lemon

3 Tbsp extra virgin olive oil

1 clove garlic, crushed

10 g/$\frac{1}{4}$ oz mint, chopped
 plus extra to garnish

salt and freshly ground
 black pepper

50 g/2 oz pine nuts, toasted
 (optional)

Serves 4–6

1. Heat the barbecue or griddle pan to medium-hot. Brush the courgette slices with a little olive oil and put as many as you can in a single layer on the barbecue or griddle. Leave to cook for 1–2 minutes on each side, or until charred and cooked. Remove and set aside, repeating until all the slices are cooked. Leave the courgette slices to cool slightly while you prepare the dressing.

2. Whisk the lemon juice, olive oil, garlic and mint together and season generously with salt and pepper. Pour the dressing over the still warm courgettes and gently combine.

This salad can be served warm or left to marinate for up to 24 hours. Just before serving top with extra mint and toasted pine nuts, if liked.

Fattoush

2–3 soft flour tortillas

2 Tbsp olive oil

For the dressing:

3 Tbsp red wine vinegar

4 Tbsp extra virgin olive oil

1 tsp sumac

sea salt and freshly ground
black pepper

4 red, green or yellow
tomatoes, cut into
1–2 cm/½–¾ in cubes

1 large or 2 small cucumbers,
halved lengthways then cut
into 1–2 cm/½–¾ in chunks

1 red onion, cut into
1 cm/½ in chunks

1 small handful mint, torn

1 small handful flat-leaf
parsley, torn

Serves 4

1. Preheat the barbecue or griddle pan to medium-hot. While heating, brush the tortillas generously, on both sides, with oil. Put the tortillas, one at a time, on the barbecue or in the griddle pan and cook for about 1 minute on the first side and about 30 seconds – 1 minute on the second side. Remove the tortillas and leave to cool while you prepare the dressing.

2. In a small bowl combine the vinegar, oil and sumac with a fork and season generously with salt and pepper. Put the cubed tomato, cucumber and red onion in a salad bowl. Break the tortillas into the salad and add the herbs. Pour over the dressing and toss to combine. Serve immediately, while the tortillas are still crispy.

Rice noodles and pak choy with ginger chilli soy dressing

8 baby pak choy, halved, washed and well drained

spray vegetable oil

250 g/8 oz rice vermicelli noodles, rehydrated

60 g/2 oz green spring onions, roughly chopped

120 g/4 oz carrots, peeled and shredded

120 g/4 oz yellow pepper, deseeded and cut into fine strips

For the dressing:

2 Tbsp sesame seeds, toasted

2 Tbsp fresh ginger, finely chopped

2 Tbsp red chilli, finely chopped and with seeds left in

1 clove garlic, minced

240 ml/8 fl oz soy sauce

1 Tbsp honey

½ tsp sesame oil

To make dressing, whisk all ingredients together.

Serves 4

1. Make sure the pak choy have been wash thoroughly and drained well. Spray cut side with oil and quickly cook (mark) on very hot open grill. I do this by putting the stalk part onto the grill but allow the leaves to hang over the edge and in that way, the softer green leaves do not get dried out and burnt.

2. Lift from the grill and sit around a large round platter with the grilled part in the centre of the plate.

3. Mix the noodles, spring onions, carrots and capsicum with half the dressing. Spoon onto the platter so that the noodles overlap some of the pak choy. Spoon the remaining dressing around and over the pak choy. Sprinkle with sesame seeds and serve immediately.

Grilled corn on the cob with lime butter

For the lime butter:

150 g/5 oz butter, softened

finely grated rind of 2 limes

freshly ground black pepper, to taste

sea salt, to taste

4 corn cobs, husks on

Serves 4

1. Prepare the lime butter well in advance. Put the butter, lime rind, pepper and salt in a food processor and pulse until well blended. Lay out a large piece of foil, about 25 cm/ 10 in square, on a flat surface and put the butter in a log shape, in the centre. Roll up the foil, shaping the butter into an even log shape, and twist the ends to secure it. Refrigerate the butter for at least 4 hours or, if time is limited, freeze for about 45 minutes. If cutting the butter from frozen make sure you warm the knife slightly first.

2. Preheat the barbecue or griddle pan to medium.

3. Peel back the husks from the corn cobs (do not remove) and discard the silks. Replace the husks and soak in cold water for 10–15 minutes.

4. Place the corn directly on the grill and cook, turning 2–3 times, for 25 minutes. Allow to cool slightly. Peel back the husks and discard. Serve the corn cobs with the lime butter.

Pizza with tomatoes and chèvre pesto

Pizza base dough
(*see* page 298)

6 plum tomatoes, thinly sliced,
or 6 bunches of vine cherry
tomatoes, charred if liked

Olive oil for brushing

For the chèvre pesto:

2 cloves garlic

2 large handfuls basil leaves

4 Tbsp pine nuts, toasted

6–7 Tbsp olive oil

100 g/3½ oz soft fresh chèvre
(goat's cheese)

Salt and pepper, to taste

Prepare the pizza dough as
directed (*see* page 298).

Makes 6 x 20 cm/8 in pizzas

1. Make the pesto by combining the garlic, basil and pine nuts in a food processor. Pulse until chopped. Slowly add the oil and pulse until smooth. Add the chèvre and stir with a fork until smooth. Season with salt and pepper. Set aside with the tomatoes.

2. Preheat the barbecue to high on one side, warm on the other. Brush one side of the dough with olive oil. Pick up one round of dough with both hands and place oiled-side down, on the hot side of the barbecue. Grill until grill marks appear on the surface, 2–3 minutes. Flip the dough over and arrange the pesto and tomatoes on the cooked side. When the bottom has browned, slide the pizza to the cooler side of the barbecue. Close the lid and grill the pizza until the toppings are hot, and the cheese has melted. Transfer the pizza to a chopping board, and continue with next round of dough. Cut the pizza and serve.

Grilled antipasti

1–2 aubergines, about 500 g/9 oz sliced into 1 cm/½ in rings

3 plum tomatoes

2 courgettes, green and yellow, sliced into rings

1 red pepper

1 yellow pepper

1 large onion, peeled and sliced into 1 cm/½ in rings

2 cloves garlic

olive oil, for brushing

2 Tbsp red wine vinegar

4 Tbsp capers, drained and rinsed

1 handful basil, roughly chopped

1 handful flat-leaf parsley, roughly chopped

1 tsp sugar

salt and pepper, to taste

Serves 4–6

1. Preheat the barbecue or griddle pan to hot.

2. Place the aubergine slices on a cooling rack or in a colander and sprinkle with salt. Leave for 30 minutes, then rinse and pat dry with kitchen paper. Salting the aubergines in this way draws out all the bitter juices.

3. Brush the aubergine slices, tomatoes, courgettes, peppers, onion and garlic with oil. With a large bowl on hand, grill the vegetables in batches, until softened and grill marks appear.

4. Transfer the vegetables to a chopping board, roughly chop and place in a bowl. Add the remaining ingredients, toss and leave to cool and infuse at room temperature for 30 minutes.

Aubergine toasties

2 medium aubergines, sliced

olive oil

150 g/5 oz fresh bocconcini
mozzarella balls in whey, drained,
patted dry and sliced not too thickly

soft butter

1 loaf grainy bread, sliced toast
thickness

4 medium vine-ripened tomatoes

130 g/4½ oz rocket leaves

1 cup small basil leaves

extra virgin olive oil

½ juicy lemon

sea salt and freshly ground black
pepper

1 clove garlic, peeled and crushed
and Dijon mustard (optional)

chilli jam or fruity chutney

Serves 6

1. Dunk aubergine slices in olive oil
and cook on a barbecue hot plate
until well browned (this is important
– if they aren't cooked through they
will taste astringent). Transfer them
to a large plate as they are done,
sandwiching two slices of aubergine
together with two slices of mozzarella
cheese in the middle.

2. Meanwhile, butter 12 slices of
bread on one side only. When all
aubergine is cooked, scrape
barbecue plate as clean as possible
and lower heat. Slice tomatoes and
dress rocket leaves and basil with a
little extra virgin olive oil, a few squirts
of lemon juice, some sea salt and
black pepper. Add a little crushed
garlic and a dab of Dijon mustard if
you like.

3. Put half the bread, buttered side
down, on a board and spread with
chilli jam or chutney. Put the
aubergine and mozzarella bundles
on the bread, season with salt and
pepper and top with balance of
bread, buttered side up.

4. Cook toasties over a medium heat
on a barbecue hot plate until bread
is golden, then flip over and cook
other side. Using a metal spatula or
similar, press down on toasties once
or twice while cooking. Transfer to a
chopping board. They're delicious as
they are, but a few slices of tomato
tucked into the sandwiches along
with some of the dressed rocket and
basil leaves makes a tasty addition.
Alternatively, serve tomatoes and
leaves separately. Serve hot or
hottish, cut into halves or triangles.
There may well be extra aubergine
bundles – in which case, just butter
some more bread!

Salads and sides

Green tomato, avocado and orange salad

2 medium-sized red onions

4 ½ Tbsp extra virgin olive oil

salt and freshly ground black pepper

4 oranges

2 Tbsp lime juice

1 tsp creamy Dijon mustard

2 cloves garlic, peeled and finely chopped

pinch of sugar

1 large perfectly ripe avocado

6 medium green tomatoes

60 g/2 oz black olives, stoned

30 g/1 oz chopped coriander

Serves 4

1. Peel and cut red onions into pieces through the roots. Mix in a bowl with 1 ½ tablespoons of extra virgin olive oil and plenty of black pepper. Cook over a medium heat on a barbecue hot plate until lightly golden, then transfer to a plate.

2. Peel oranges with a serrated knife, removing and discarding all white pith, then slice into rounds. Put them in a bowl with any juice.

3. In a bowl mix the rest of the oil, lime juice, mustard, garlic and sugar with ½ teaspoon of salt and black pepper to taste.

4. Halve avocado, remove stone and slip off skin. Slice avocado flesh thickly. Slice tomatoes.

5. Arrange oranges, tomatoes, onions, avocado and olives in a salad bowl or on a platter. Scatter coriander over and pour dressing on. Toss gently and serve.

Mesclun leaves with goat cheese and barbecued garlic dressing

4 plum tomatoes

220 g/7 oz mesclun leaves (mixed baby salad leaves)

125 g/4 oz dry goat's cheese, crumbled or diced

125 ml/4 fl oz barbecued garlic dressing (*see* recipe page 283), to serve

Serves 4

1. Cut tomatoes in half. Arrange leaves in a salad bowl and top with crumbled goat cheese. (Remove the crusty skin of the cheese if you wish, but I like to leave it on.)

2. Spray tomatoes with oil and cook on the open grill for one-and-a-half minutes on each side. Lift from the barbecue and allow to cool for 10 minutes.

3. Scatter tomatoes over salad leaves and serve. Pass the barbecued garlic dressing separately.

Pink grapefruit and avocado salad

1 tsp olive oil

60 g/2 oz pine nuts

sea salt

3 pink grapefruit

1 Tbsp extra virgin olive oil

1 Tbsp manuka or fragrant honey, warmed

salt and freshly ground black pepper

1 ripe but firm avocado

130 g/4½ oz bag Cos lettuce leaves or 1 small Cos lettuce, washed, dried and torn into bite-sized pieces

mint leaves

Serves 4

1. Heat olive oil in a small frying pan or saucepan and add pine nuts. Cook, stirring often, until golden. Transfer to a plate lined with absorbent kitchen paper and sprinkle with sea salt.

2. Using a small serrated knife, peel grapefruit. Remove and discard pith. Cut flesh into segments, then squeeze juice into a small bowl.

3. Whisk extra virgin olive oil, honey and 1 tablespoon of grapefruit juice with ¼ teaspoon of salt and black pepper to taste (drink the rest of the juice!).

4. Halve avocado, remove stone, then peel and slice flesh. Arrange cos leaves on a serving platter and top with grapefruit segments, slices of avocado, mint leaves and pine nuts. Rewhisk dressing and spoon it over salad. Serve immediately.

Chicory, walnut and pear salad

2–3 heads chicory

50 ml/2 fl oz + 1 Tbsp extra virgin olive oil

2–3 ripe pears

Juice of 2 lemons

Salt and freshly ground black pepper

75 g/2¾ oz walnuts, toasted

Serves 4-6

1. Cut the ends of the chicory and pull the leaves to separate them. Put the chicory in a bowl with 1 Tbsp oil and toss to coat.

2. Heat the barbecue hot plate or griddle pan to medium and cook the chicory, turning frequently, for 2–3 minutes, or until wilted and slightly charred. Transfer to a serving plate and leave to cool slightly while you prepare the rest of the salad.

3. Cut the pears in half then core and slice thinly. Combine the lemon juice, 50 ml/2 fl oz extra virgin olive oil, salt and pepper and pour over the pears. Toss gently to coat and stop browning. Pour the pears and all of the dressing over the chicory. Sprinkle over the walnuts and an extra grinding of black pepper and serve.

Barbecued potato salad with anchovy and garlic dressing

400 g/14 oz kipfler potatoes (Pink Fir Apple or baby Desiree will do too)

olive oil spray

3 green spring onions, white only and finely sliced

2 hard-boiled eggs, shells removed and roughly chopped

2 Tbsp crisp bacon pieces

3 Tbsp mint, roughly chopped

4 anchovy fillets, drained well

4 cloves garlic, poached for 5 minutes

120 ml/4 fl oz good mayonnaise

60 ml/4 fl oz white vinegar

½ tsp ground black pepper

Serves 4

1. Cut the potatoes on the diagonal into bite-sized pieces. Boil in salted water for 5 minutes – drain well and cool. When cool enough to handle, spray with oil and cook until tender on a medium–hot open grill.

2. Remove from the barbecue and tip into large mixing bowl. Add the spring onions, eggs, bacon and mint.

3. Mash the anchovies with the garlic. Stir in the mayonnaise, vinegar and ground black pepper to taste and pour over the potato mixture.

4. Toss to coat the ingredients and leave to cool. Refrigerate to use when needed.

Seared lamb loin salad

350 g/12 oz lamb loin

vegetable oil, for brushing

For the marinade:

2 shallots, thinly sliced

2 Tbsp chopped mint

2 Tbsp chopped coriander

2 Tbsp finely chopped fresh ginger

1 red finger chilli pepper, deseeded and finely chopped

juice and grated rind of 2 limes

2 tsp fish sauce

4 Tbsp soy sauce

For the salad:

200 g/7 oz mixed salad leaves

1 tsp sesame oil

Parmesan cheese shavings, to serve

sea salt and pepper, to taste

Serves 4

1. Preheat the barbecue or griddle pan to hot. Brush the lamb loin with oil and grill until a deep brown colour, 2–3 minutes on all four sides. Allow to cool slightly.

2. Combine all the marinade ingredients in a shallow baking dish. Place the lamb in the marinade and turn to coat. Cover and refrigerate for 2–3 hours, turning occasionally. Remove the lamb from the marinade and thinly slice. Place the salad leaves in a bowl and toss with sesame oil and a spoonful of the lamb marinade. Place the salad on a serving platter, and fan the sliced lamb on top. Scatter with Parmesan shavings and finish off with a sprinkling of sea salt and pepper and a drizzle of marinade.

Smoked vegetarian Caesar salad

For the Caesar dressing:
100 g/3 ½ oz silken tofu
2 Tbsp lemon juice
2 tsp Dijon mustard
1 clove garlic, crushed
¼ tsp salt
1 pinch sugar
dash Worcestershire sauce
2 Tbsp grated Parmesan
freshly ground pepper, to taste
2 heads Cos lettuce, outer leaves removed
Parmesan shavings, to garnish.

1 handful wood chips, soaked for 1 hour.

For the crispy capers:
2 Tbsp olive oil
50 g/2 oz capers

Serves 4

1. To make the dressing, put all ingredients into a blender and blend until smooth.

2. For the crispy capers, pour the olive oil into a small saucepan and heat until hot. Add the capers and sauté until crispy. Drain the capers on kitchen paper.

3. Preheat the barbecue or griddle pan to medium-hot. If using a barbecue, scatter wood chips over the coals or place in a smoker box. Brush the grill with oil. Grill the lettuce halves, cut-side down, until warm and slightly charred, about 2 minutes. Divide between four salad plates. Top with dressing, crispy capers and shavings of Parmesan.

Barbecued pear with pancetta, gorgonzola and spinach salad

2 Beurre Bosch pears

1 lemon, halved

125 g/4 oz gorgonzola, crumbled or diced

220 g/7 oz spinach leaves, washed, stems removed, crisped

8 slices pancetta

saffron threads

2 Tbsp extra virgin olive oil

1 Tbsp red wine vinegar

Serves 4

1. Halve pears lengthwise and remove stems and seeds. (This is best done with a Parisienne cutter and a sharp knife.) Slice pears into lengths 1 cm/½ in thick. If you are not doing the barbecuing immediately, rub each slice with lemon to prevent browning. Put cheese and spinach leaves in a salad bowl, cover and refrigerate.

2. Cook pancetta on the open grill, turning regularly, until crisp. The pears must be 'flash' barbecued, just to bring out some extra flavour, so spray the slices with the smallest amount of oil and cook them on the open grill for just 30 seconds on each side. Lift pears from the barbecue to a warm platter and sprinkle immediately with two good pinches of saffron threads. Take pears and pancetta to the kitchen and arrange on top of the cheese and spinach.

3. Drizzle the salad with olive oil and red wine vinegar and serve at once.

Green papaya salad

410 g/13 oz of fresh green
papaya, finely shredded

120 g/4 oz fresh mint leaves,
washed

120 g/4 oz fresh coriander
leaves, washed

120 g/4 oz snipped
garlic chives

1 Tbsp finely shredded Kaffir
lime leaves

1 Tbsp red chilli, seeded and
finely diced

125 ml/4 fl oz nam jim dressing
(*see* recipe page 284)

Serves 4

1. Combine all ingredients and stir well.
Serve immediately.

King prawn caesar salad

For the dressing:

3 anchovy fillets, well drained of oil

2 egg yolks

2 large cloves garlic, minced

1 tsp Worcestershire sauce

1 Tbsp white vinegar

120 ml olive oil

For the salad:

24 medium sized green king prawns, peeled with tails on, de-veined and butterflied

oil spray

120 g/4 oz cos lettuce, inner whiter leaves, washed, crisped and cut into bite-sized pieces

2 hard boiled eggs, shelled and roughly chopped

4 Tbsp crisp bacon bits

50 g/1½ oz shaved parmesan cheese

garlic croutons to taste

For the garlic croutons:

4 slices day-old sourdough bread

1 Tbsp garlic, crushed and mixed with 2 Tbsp olive oil

Serves 4

1. Make the dressing in the bowl in which you will serve the salad. Mash the anchovies with the back of a fork and add the egg yolks, garlic, Worcestershire and vinegar. Combine until lighter in colour and thickened. Whisk in the oil slowly to make a thick dressing.

2. Spray the prawns with oil and cook on medium-hot flat plate. Toss to cook through then remove and cool. Add the lettuce, eggs, bacon and cooled prawns to the dressing and toss to coat, then sprinkle on the cheese and croutons. Serve in the middle of table.

Garlic croutons:

1. Cut the bread into 2cm squares. Heat the garlic oil to medium-hot in an ovenproof pan. Toss in the bread cubes and coat with the oil mixture. Put into a moderate oven until browned. Tip onto absorbant paper when done. They keep very well in an airtight container.

Charred red peppers with anchovies

4 red peppers

mandarin-infused extra virgin olive oil

250 g/8 oz cherry tomatoes

4 cloves garlic, peeled and crushed

handful of basil leaves

150 g/5 oz feta cheese, crumbled

salt and freshly ground black pepper

8 anchovies in olive oil, drained

2 Tbsp balsamic vinegar

Serves 4-8

1. Halve the peppers and remove seeds and soft membrane without disturbing the cores (cores will hold peppers together and stop filling spilling out). Rub peppers all over with mandarin-infused olive oil.

2. In a bowl mix together cherry tomatoes, garlic, basil, feta, and a little salt and pepper and spoon into the peppers. Top each with an anchovy and drizzle with a little balsamic vinegar and a tiny drizzle of the mandarin-infused oil.

3. Cook peppers over a medium heat on a double sheet of aluminium foil on a barbecue hot plate with the hood down for about 15 minutes or until peppers and contents are hot and starting to wilt a little and the bottom of the peppers are starting to char. If you have a top grill, flash peppers under it until crisp (or finish them off under an oven grill). Peppers can also be cooked in an oven preheated to 200° C/400° F (gas 6) for about 15 minutes (or until feta has browned on top).

Baked potatoes, peppers and chorizo

2 red and 2 yellow peppers

about 4–6 large floury potatoes, peeled and roughly cut into fat fingers

salt and freshly ground black pepper to taste

3 Tbsp extra virgin olive oil

3 fresh chorizo sausages

2 Tbsp fresh rosemary leaves

Serves 4

1. Halve peppers, remove cores and seeds and cut each half into three pieces. Put potatoes and peppers in a large shallow roasting tin. Season with salt and pepper and drizzle with oil.

2. Cook vegetables for about 1 hour in an oven preheated to 200° C/400° F (gas 6), turning them over once or twice, or until golden and crisp.

3. Meanwhile, cook chorizo sausages over a medium heat on an oiled barbecue hot plate for a few minutes or until cooked through. Slice thickly, then add sausages along with the rosemary to the roasting dish containing potatoes and peppers. Cook for a further 5 minutes, then transfer to a serving dish. Serve hot.

Button mushrooms with thyme

500 g/1 lb very firm snow-white or brown button mushrooms, wiped clean and halved if large

4 Tbsp extra virgin olive oil

several sprigs thyme

8 small fresh bay leaves

finely grated zest of 1 lemon

salt and freshly ground black pepper

Serves 6

1. Put mushrooms in a bowl, pour on the oil and add thyme, bay leaves, lemon zest and pepper. Stir well to coat.

2. Cook on a very hot barbecue hot plate, turning often, until they are golden brown; don't overcook – they should be well browned but not soft. Transfer mushrooms to a side plate, toss through some salt and serve immediately.

Aubergine stack with asparagus

500 g/1 lb plump asparagus, trimmed

olive oil

sea salt and freshly ground black pepper

2 medium-large aubergines

salt

3–4 large beefsteak tomatoes

handful of basil leaves

3 Tbsp extra virgin olive oil

aged balsamic vinegar

2 cloves garlic, peeled and crushed

Serves 4

1. Put asparagus in a flat dish, drizzle with olive oil and season with sea salt and pepper. Toss gently to coat spears with oil.

2. Cook asparagus over a hot barbecue grill rack for a few minutes on each side until lightly charred but crunchy, turning with tongs. Alternatively, cook in an oven preheated to 200° C/400° F (gas 6) until spears caramelize and tips turn crunchy. Asparagus can be cooked up to 2 hours ahead. Slice asparagus on the diagonal, reserving tips for garnishing. Split tips in half lengthways.

Slice aubergines into rounds. Dunk slices in olive oil and cook over a medium-high heat on a barbecue hot plate until very tender and a deep golden brown. Transfer to a plate and season with salt.

3. Cut tomatoes into thick slices, pat dry with absorbent kitchen paper and cook on a very hot oiled barbecue hot plate until lightly coloured; don't overcook. Arrange cooked tomatoes and aubergine in stacks, putting sliced asparagus and some of the basil leaves in between, on individual plates. Arrange asparagus spears on top.

4. Have ready a dressing made with the extra virgin olive oil, a few splashes of aged balsamic vinegar, garlic, 1/4 teaspoon salt and some black pepper and torn basil leaves. Spoon over the stacks and serve immediately.

Baby leeks with oregano dressing

16 baby leeks

For the oregano dressing:

1 red shallot, peeled and very finely chopped

2 Tbsp sherry vinegar

2 Tbsp walnut oil

1 Tbsp oregano, roughly chopped

white pepper

olive oil spray

sea salt

2 tomatoes, flesh only, and julienned

oregano sprigs for decoration

Serves 4

1. Trim the leeks to around 15 cm/6 in in length, removing all excess green parts. Peel off the outside layer of the leeks and ensure the root parts are trimmed. Whisk together the shallot, vinegar, oil and chopped oregano, adding pepper to taste, to make the dressing. Place the leeks in the oregano dressing to marinate and allow to cool. Then cover and set aside for at least two hours. While it's preferable to have the leeks at room temperature, if you are not using them within two hours, store them in the refrigerator.

2. Spray the leeks with oil and position them on the barbecue so they sit across the slats at right angles. Sprinkle with a little salt and cook until they soften; leeks lose their crispness if cooked right through. Test the leeks by inserting a skewer to check how firm they are in the centre. When cooked, remove the leeks and return to the kitchen.

3. Place the leeks on individual plates; sprinkle over the julienned tomatoes and decorate with oregano sprigs. Spoon on any extra dressing.

Barbecued nectarine wedges, pancetta and feta salad

2 large nectarines, just ripe

120 ml/4 fl oz vanilla olive oil

1 tsp Dijon mustard

2 Tbsp white wine vinegar

olive oil spray

8–12 slices pancetta

4 x 2 cm/¾ in slices
   Cinnamon courgette bread
   (*see* recipe page 299)

salad greens

200 g/7 oz feta cheese,
   crumbled

Serves 4

1. Wash the nectarines and halve, then cut the halves into wedges. Make the dressing by whisking together the oil and mustard; when combined, whisk in the vinegar. Set aside but do not refrigerate.

2. Spray the nectarine wedges with oil and place on the open slats. Cook the nectarine wedges quickly, turning them regularly and remove when they are well marked. At the same time, cook the pancetta on the flat plate. When crisped and browned, remove to a plate lined with paper kitchen towel. Spray the bread with oil and brown both sides on the open slats.

3. Place salad greens in a large bowl, top with the nectarine wedges and feta cheese, crumble over the crispy pancetta and add the dressing. Serve the Cinnamon courgette bread separately.

Asparagus wrapped in Parma ham

24 asparagus spears

150 g/5 oz (about 12) Parma ham slices, halved

Extra virgin olive oil

Freshly ground black pepper

Serves 4–6

1. Snap the ends off the asparagus where they break naturally and trim the ends on a diagonal.

2. Wrap half a slice of Parma ham around the centre of each asparagus spear. Preheat the barbecue or griddle pan to medium-hot and cook all the asparagus spears at once, drizzle over a little oil while cooking and season with plenty of freshly ground black pepper, for about 3–4 minutes, turning once or twice. The ham will go crispy and golden brown and the asparagus will turn bright green. Serve hot, warm or cold.

Chargrilled skewered new potatoes

1 kg/2 lb medium new
  potatoes, washed and
  unpeeled

4 Tbsp olive oil

sea salt and freshly ground
  black pepper

bamboo skewers, pre-soaked
  in cold water for 1 hour

Serves 4

1. Cook the potatoes in boiling salted water until just tender, about 15 minutes. Drain the potatoes and allow to cool. Cut the potatoes in half and toss gently in a bowl with the olive oil and seasonings. Thread the potatoes onto the skewers and grill on a medium heat until heated and lightly charred.

Desserts

Blueberry buttermilk pancakes

4 medium eggs

475 ml/8 fl oz buttermilk

100 g/3½ oz butter, melted and cooled

350 g/12½ oz self-raising flour

5 Tbsp caster sugar

finely grated zest of 2 lemons and juice of 1 lemon

400 g/14 oz fresh or frozen blueberries

Greek yoghurt for serving

Serves 16–20 Pancakes

1. In a large bowl whisk together eggs and buttermilk, then whisk in cooled butter. Sift in flour and stir in 4 tablespoons of the sugar. Fold in lemon zest and 300 g/10 oz of blueberries; don't stir because this will turn the batter blue.

2. Cook pancakes over a medium heat on a lightly oiled barbecue hot plate until golden brown. Flip them over and cook other side until golden. Keep them warm on a plate covered with a clean tea towel while cooking remaining pancakes.

3. Alternatively, heat a large non-stick frying pan over a medium heat. Lightly oil pan. Add tablespoonfuls of batter, spreading it out slightly, leaving enough room for pancakes to spread (cook in batches of three). Cook for 3–4 minutes or until pancakes are golden brown underneath. Turn pancakes over with a spatula and cook other side until light brown.

4. Put remaining blueberries in a saucepan with 1 tablespoon of sugar and the juice of 1 lemon. Cook gently for about 2–3 minutes. Serve pancakes with blueberry syrup and Greek yoghurt.

Caramelized fruit kebabs

Fruit – choose from any combination of bananas, kiwifruit, pineapple, peaches, nectarines or strawberries or other firm fruits

Cointreau liqueur or a liqueur or spirit of your choice

icing sugar

butter

bamboo skewers, soaked in cold water for 30 minutes

Allow 3 skewers per person

1. Prepare fruit by peeling, hulling or deseeding as appropriate, then cut into small chunks. Thread fruit onto skewers, placing them on a plate as they are done. Sprinkle over a little liqueur and leave to macerate for 10 minutes, turning from time to time. Sieve a little icing sugar onto a plate.

2. Heat the barbecue to medium-high and when ready to cook the fruit, butter the hot plate. Quickly pass kebabs through the icing sugar then put them on the hot plate. Cook for 1–2 minutes on each side or until the sugar is slightly caramelized. Serve immediately.

3. Alternatively, heat a non-stick frying pan large enough to accommodate skewers over a medium heat. When it is hot drop in a little butter, which should sizzle and foam but not burn. Add the kebabs and cook until caramelised. Serve immediately. (Pour water into pan to lift off caramelized sugar.)

Grilled s'mores sandwiches

4 slices brioche

6 large marshmallows

100 g/3½ oz milk chocolate, broken into chunks

Butter, softened

Serves 2

1. Preheat the barbecue or griddle pan to medium-hot. Place the brioche slices on a chopping board. Divide the marshmallows between two pieces of brioche. Place the chocolate on top of the marshmallows. Top with the remaining brioche slices. Butter the top brioche slices.

2. Carefully invert the sandwiches on to the grill bars. Grill, pressing gently with a spatula, until the insides begin to melt and grill marks appear on the surface. Flip over, grill for a further minute then transfer the sandwiches to a cooler part of the grill and continue to grill until the insides have completely melted, a further 1–2 minutes.

3. Transfer to plates and serve immediately.

If brioche is unavailable, substitute another slightly sweet bread, such as Chollah.

Bananas with rum and whipped mascarpone

220 g/7 oz mascarpone

60 ml/2 fl oz pouring cream

2 Tbsp vanilla sugar

8 bananas, each about
  90 g/3 oz, not too ripe,
  peeled

60 g/2 oz butter, melted

60 ml/2 fl oz dark rum

Serves 4

1. Whip mascarpone with cream and vanilla sugar.

2. Spread half the melted butter on the flat plate and cook bananas for two minutes. Spoon remaining melted butter over and, using a long spatula and a set of tongs, turn over the bananas gently and cook for two minutes more. Lift onto a platter.

3. Pour rum over the bananas and serve with the whipped mascarpone.

Marsala-poached and griddled pears

250 g/8 oz caster sugar

200 ml/7 fl oz Marsala

300 ml/10 fl oz water

1 Tbsp black peppercorns

6 Conference pears, skin removed

200 g/7 oz Gorgonzola cheese

100 g/3½ oz shelled walnut halves, toasted

Serves 6

1. Put the sugar, Marsala, water and peppercorns in a large saucepan and bring to the boil, over high heat, stirring until the sugar is dissolved. Add the pears and enough water to just cover them. Bring back to the boil, reduce the heat and simmer for about 20 minutes, or until the pears are tender but still firm. Remove the pears and set aside. Bring the liquid back to the boil and leave to simmer until it has reduced to a syrup, about 45 minutes. Pour the syrup over the pears and leave to cool completely.

2. When you are ready to serve, preheat the griddle pan to medium. Halve and core the pears and place cut-side down on the griddle pan for 2–3 minutes, or until the griddle pan has left a decorative griddle mark on them, then turn over and cook on the second side for a further 1–2 minutes. Remove from the pan and place two pear halves on each plate. Add a generous chunk of Gorgonzola on the side, sprinkle over the walnuts and, finally, drizzle all over with the syrup. Serve immediately with some crisp crackers and a glass of Marsala or sweet dessert wine on the side, if liked.

Strawberry crêpes with mango cream

16 medium-size strawberries, hulls removed, halved

30 g/1 oz caster sugar

60 ml/2 fl oz Grand Marnier, or Cointreau

1 large mango, very ripe

250 ml/8 fl oz thickened cream

4 crêpes

icing sugar, for dusting

For the crêpe batter (makes 20 to 24 crêpes):

345 g/11 oz plain flour

pinch of salt

3 eggs, beaten

375 ml/12 fl oz milk

1 Tbsp brandy

2 tsp butter, melted

extra butter, for greasing pan

Serves 4

1. Sprinkle strawberries with sugar and Grand Marnier and leave to macerate for at least one hour. Remove skin from the mango and slice the flesh away from the seed. Purée very finely in a food processor. Whip the cream until stiff, stir in mango purée and refrigerate. To make the crêpes, sift flour and salt into a bowl. Make a well in the centre and add eggs and milk. Using a balloon whisk, mix well, drawing in the flour from the sides of the well. Beat until smooth, then stir in brandy and melted butter; cover and stand for one hour. Strain into a jug.

2. To cook the crêpes, heat a little butter in an 18 cm/7 in crêpe pan and pour off excess. Pour about 1 tablespoon of batter from the jug into the pan, rotating the pan quickly to coat bottom thinly and evenly. Pour off any excess batter. Heat gently and, when small bubbles appear, use a spatula to flip the crêpe over. Cook for another minute on the second side. Repeat until all batter is used. Keep four crêpes warm, and cool the remainder on wire racks.

3. Lift strawberry halves from the liquid with a slotted spoon and place on the flat plate (it is not necessary to spray the flat plate). Turn very quickly, warming for no longer than one minute in total. Lift the strawberries from the plate and place eight halves down the centre of each crêpe. Loosely fold crêpes around the strawberries.

4. Spoon remaining liqueur soaking liquid over crêpes, dust with icing sugar and serve with the mango cream.

Apricot skewers with almond blancmange

For the almond blancmange:

475 ml/16fl oz milk

1 tsp lemon zest, finely grated

2 Tbsp almond meal

4 Tbsp cornflour

2 Tbsp caster sugar

¼ tsp almond essence

12–16 apricots, only just ripe

4–8 metal skewers, depending on the size of the apricots and the skewers

120 ml/4 fl oz Drambuie

2 Tbsp caster sugar

icing sugar for dusting

Serves 4

1. To make the blancmange, reserve 2 fl oz of milk and pour the rest into a non-stick saucepan; place over medium heat and add the lemon zest and almond meal. Stir until it almost boils then remove from heat. In a bowl, mix the cornflour and sugar with the reserved milk and stir to a paste. Then add a cupful of the heated milk and stir before pouring it all back into the saucepan of heated milk. Add the almond essence and return to the heat, stirring until the mixture is simmering. Simmer for 3 minutes. Pour into a wet mould, or four individual ones, cool and refrigerate for at least 4 hours for the blancmange to set.

2. Cut the apricots in half, horizontally and discard the stones. Thread the apricot halves onto the skewers so that when the skewers are laid down, the apricots are cut-side up and look like joined circles. Place the skewers on a plate, sprinkle with half the Drambuie and leave for at least 1 hour. Sprinkle the cut sides of the apricots with caster sugar and a little more Drambuie; place the skewers on the barbecue cut-side down and only just heat them through. The apricots cook quickly because of their natural sugars as well as the added sugar, and will be marked by the open slats. Turn the apricots over onto their skin side and leave for around 30 seconds. Remove apricots and put on a platter cut-side up. Sprinkle with additional Drambuie.

3. Remove the blancmange from the mould, or smaller moulds. Place the mould in very hot water. As soon as you can see just the smallest amount of liquid forming around the inside of the mould, invert the mould onto a plate. If you are using individual moulds, place a blancmange on each plate and add a skewer or two of apricots. Add more Drambuie if desired, then drench with a good dusting of icing sugar.

Sambuca mango cheeks and minted crème fraîche

4 medium mangoes, ripe but not mushy

220 g/8 oz crème fraîche

2 Tbsp honey

2 Tbsp ripped mint leaves (spearmint if possible)

1 Tbsp icing sugar

60 ml/2 fl oz white Sambuca

Serves 4

1. Cut the cheeks from the mangoes and cut square shapes into the cheeks without cutting through the skin. At least 3 hours before use, mix the crème fraîche with the honey and mint leaves. Refrigerate until ready to serve.

2. Sprinkle the cut side of the mango cheeks with equal amounts of icing sugar and set aside until the sugar melts. Place the cheeks on the open slats to cook for a minute – the cheeks will brown very quickly, so turn them gently as you want to retain the marks of the open slats. A long spatula works well here. Leave the cheeks on the open slats for 30 seconds then transfer them to a plate.

3. Place the mango cheeks on a platter and spoon the Sambuca over them. Serve with the crème fraîche in a separate bowl.

Roasted rhubarb with ginger syrup

6 stalks rhubarb, about 600 g/1lb 4 oz, cut into 4 cm/ 1½ in lengths

4 pieces stem ginger, finely chopped

4 Tbsp stem ginger syrup

Vanilla yoghurt, ice cream or whipped cream, to serve

Serves 4

1. Preheat the barbecue to medium-hot, or preheat the oven to 180° C/350° F (gas 4).

2. Take two sheets of foil, each 40 cm/16 in long, and place one sheet on top of the other. Place the chopped rhubarb in the middle of the foil and toss with stem ginger and syrup. Bring the edges of the foil together and fold, creating an airtight package.

3. Place the foil package directly on the grill, cover and leave for 10–15 minutes until the rhubarb is cooked through. Spoon the rhubarb over vanilla yoghurt, ice cream or simple whipped cream.

Caramelized oranges on brioche

4 oranges, skin removed and halved crosswise

2 Tbsp demerara sugar

3 Tbsp brandy

4 slices brioche

mint leaves, to serve (optional)

For the mascarpone cream:

100 g/3½ oz mascarpone

100 g/3½ oz crème fraîche

50 g/2 oz demerara sugar

1 tsp vanilla extract

Serves 4

1. Put the oranges in a flat dish, cut-side up. Sprinkle over the sugar. Drizzle over the brandy, cover and chill for 1–2 hours.

2. While the oranges are chilling prepare the mascarpone cream, which also requires chilling time. Combine all the ingredients in a bowl, mix until well combined and refrigerate until you are ready to serve, at least 1 hour.

3. Heat the barbecue hot plate (not grill plate) or griddle pan to medium-hot and cook the brioche slices for about 30 seconds – 1 minute on each side, or until just golden, and transfer to serving plates. Then cook the oranges, cut-side down, for about 4–5 minutes, pouring over the extra juices after 2–3 minutes. Move the oranges around in the syrup, turning once or twice, until dark brown, sticky and caramelized. Spread the mascarpone cream over the cooked brioche slices and top with the oranges and any juices. Serve warm with a mint leaf on top, if liked.

Barbecue basics

Red pepper sauce

3 red peppers

1 large onion, peeled and chopped

2 large cloves garlic, peeled and crushed

125 ml/4 fl oz white wine

125 ml/4 fl oz cider vinegar

750 ml/24 fl oz olive oil

2 Tbsp roughly chopped fresh thyme leaves

¼ tsp salt

cayenne pepper, optional

Makes about 1.5 L/40 fl oz

Remove the seeds and cores from the pepper and chop the flesh finely. Place in saucepan with remaining ingredients, except cayenne pepper. Bring to the boil and simmer for one-and-a-quarter hours. Purée in a food processor or blender and strain. Taste and adjust seasoning, adding a little cayenne pepper if you like. Pour into sterilized jars and cool. Keeps, refrigerated, for two weeks.

Homemade barbecue sauce

30 g/1 oz garlic cloves, peeled

250 ml/8 fl oz orange juice

250 ml/8 fl oz tomato sauce

250 ml/8 fl oz red wine

125 ml/4 fl oz golden syrup, or maple syrup

60 ml/2 fl oz malt vinegar

60 g/2 oz onion, chopped

Makes about 1 L/32 fl oz

Spray the flat plate lightly with oil, and cook garlic for four minutes, turning constantly to brown it lightly. Remove from the heat.

Purée garlic with remaining ingredients in a food processor or blender. Pour into a saucepan and simmer for 15–20 minutes, or until reduced to the consistency of commercial tomato sauce.

Serve warm. Keeps, refrigerated, for about two weeks.

Sweet Thai chilli sauce

4 cloves garlic, roughly chopped

2 large red chilli peppers, stems removed

2 tsp grated fresh ginger

grated rind of 2 limes

2 stalks lemongrass, roughly chopped

10 g/¼ oz coriander leaves and stalks

200 g/7 oz caster sugar

75 ml/2½ fl oz cider vinegar

3 Tbsp fish sauce

3 Tbsp light soy sauce

Makes 350 ml/12 fl oz

Purée the first six ingredients to a paste in a food processor. Put the sugar in a medium-sized saucepan with 3 Tbsp water and heat, stirring, until the sugar dissolves. Remove the spoon, increase the heat and boil gently for 5–6 minutes, until light golden caramel in colour. Carefully stir in the paste.

Bring back to the boil and add the vinegar, fish sauce and soy sauce. Bring back to the boil again and simmer for a further minute. Remove from the heat and leave to cool before serving. This sauce will keep for up to 1 month, stored in a sterilized, airtight jar in the fridge.

Gran's plum sauce

1.5 kg/3 lb 5 oz red plums

750 g/1 lb 10 oz brown sugar

2 tsp salt

750 ml/1½ pt white wine vinegar

1 tsp cayenne pepper

2 onions, chopped

2 apples, chopped

2 tsp allspice

1 tsp ground cloves

2.5 cm/1 in piece fresh ginger, bruised

Makes 1.5 L/3 pt

Put all the ingredients in a large saucepan and mix to combine. Bring to the boil, reduce the heat and simmer for 1½–2 hours, or until thick and pulpy. Strain the sauce through a mouli-légumes or coarse sieve and pour into sterilized jars or bottles. This sauce will keep for up to 1 month. Refrigerate after opening.

Peanut sauce

1 Tbsp peanut or groundnut oil

1 onion, finely chopped

2 cloves garlic, crushed

½–1 tsp chilli flakes

2 Tbsp dark soy sauce

1 Tbsp brown sugar

1 Tbsp tamarind paste
  or lime juice

200 g/7 oz crunchy
  peanut butter

200 ml/7 fl oz coconut milk

Makes 500 ml/18 fl oz

Heat the oil in a medium saucepan and fry the onion, garlic and chilli flakes over medium heat for 3–4 minutes but do not brown. Reduce the heat to low and stir in the soy sauce, brown sugar, tamarind paste, peanut butter and coconut milk. Bring to the boil, reduce the heat and simmer for 2–3 minutes. This sauce will keep, covered, in the fridge for up to 1 week.

Apricot bbq sauce

1 kg/2 lb ripe apricots, halved and stoned

500 g/1 lb tomatoes, halved

500 g/1 lb brown sugar

500 ml/18 fl oz cider vinegar

2 onions, peeled and chopped

2 cloves garlic

1 red chilli pepper, halved

2 Tbsp soy sauce

2 tsp Dijon mustard

2 tsp smoked paprika

Makes 1.5 L/3 pt

Put all the ingredients in a large saucepan or stockpot and mix to combine. Bring to the boil, reduce the heat and simmer for 1–1½ hours, or until thick and pulpy. Remove the chilli pepper and strain the sauce through a mouli-légumes or coarse sieve and pour into sterilized jars or bottles. This sauce will keep for up to 1 month. Refrigerate after opening.

Mustard bourbon bbq sauce

1 tsp vegetable oil

1 bunch salad onions, chopped

1 medium onion, chopped

4 large cloves garlic, chopped

200 g/7 oz packed golden brown sugar

125 ml/4 fl oz tomato ketchup

75 ml/2½ fl oz tomato purée

125 ml/4 fl oz grainy Dijon mustard

125 ml/4 fl oz water

75 ml/2½ fl oz Worcestershire sauce

75 ml/2½ fl oz cider vinegar

75 ml/2½ fl oz apple juice

1 chipotle chilli in adobo sauce, finely chopped

1 tsp ground cumin

350 ml/12 fl oz bourbon

Makes 750 ml/1½ pt

Heat the oil in a heavy, large saucepan over medium-low heat. Add the salad onions, onion and garlic and sauté until tender, about 15 minutes. Mix in the remaining ingredients, adding the bourbon last. Simmer the sauce until thick and reduced to 750 ml/1¼ pt, stirring occasionally, about 1 hour. Season to taste with salt and pepper. This sauce can be prepared 2 weeks ahead. Cover and refrigerate.

Tzatziki

200 g/7 oz Greek yogurt

½ large cucumber, deseeded and cut into small cubes

10 g/¼ oz mint, shredded

Juice of 1 lemon

Salt and freshly ground black pepper

Makes 250 ml/8 fl oz

Combine all the ingredients in a bowl and refrigerate until ready to serve. This will keep in the refrigerator for 3–4 days.

Basic handmade mayonnaise

2 large egg yolks, at room temperature

¼ tsp salt

pinch of white pepper

½ tsp prepared mustard (smooth Dijon is best)

1 tsp white vinegar

250 ml/8 fl oz light olive oil, or vegetable oil

Makes about 310 ml/10 fl oz

If you add the oil too quickly, the mayonnaise will curdle. If this happens, beat in 1 teaspoon of hot water and continue to add the oil gradually to the mixture. Remember that when you use egg yolks they cook very quickly, so if you are doing a warm egg yolk sauce, such as an hollandaise, and the egg yolks look as if they will curdle, drop a small ice cube into the mixture and whisk away from the heat.

Place egg yolks, salt, pepper, mustard and vinegar in a clean, warm mixing bowl. (Secure the bowl by wrapping a damp teatowel around its base to keep it steady on the bench. Alternatively, ask somebody to hold the bowl in place.) With a clean balloon whisk, whisk these ingredients together until light gold in colour. Whisk in the oil, almost drop by drop until you have added a third. Slowly increase the flow of oil to a thin, steady stream until all oil has been incorporated. Keeps, refrigerated, for up to six days.

Cranberry pear chutney

180 g/6 oz chopped shallots

1 Tbsp vegetable oil

350 g/12 oz bag fresh or
  frozen cranberries

2 pears, peeled, cored,
  quartered and chopped

120 g/4 oz sugar

60 ml/2¼ fl oz cider vinegar

1 tsp crushed garlic

1 tsp very finely chopped
  fresh ginger

½ tsp salt

½ tsp pepper

Makes 600 ml/1 pt

In a saucepan over medium heat sauté the shallots until softened, stirring often, about 10 minutes. Stir in the remaining ingredients and simmer, stirring occasionally, for 15 minutes, until the berries collapse. Store chutney in a sterilized, airtight jar or container for up to 2 weeks in the refrigerator or 3 months in the freezer.

Chilli jam

60 g/2 oz large Thai
  dried chillies

315 g/10 oz red Thai
  shallots, fried

155 g/5 oz garlic, fried

60 g/2 oz dried prawns

250 g/8 oz palm sugar

125 g/4 oz tamarind pulp

Makes about 1 kg/2 lb

Roast the chillies briefly in a dry frying pan.
Using a pestle and mortar or food processor,
blend all ingredients to a smooth paste.
Transfer to a saucepan and bring to the boil
over medium heat. Reduce heat and
simmer, stirring constantly as jam cooks for
five minutes.

Spoon into sterillized jars and cover with lids
when cool. It will keep, refrigerated, for a
long time.

Barbecued garlic dressing

30 g/1 oz cloves garlic

250 ml/8 fl oz light olive oil

½ tsp salt

¼ tsp freshly ground black pepper

1 tsp white sugar

2 Tbsp Spanish sherry vinegar

Makes about 310 ml/10 fl oz

If the garlic cloves are large, cut them in half.

Spray the flat plate with oil and cook garlic for four minutes, turning it regularly to allow it to brown lightly. Lift from the barbecue. Return to the kitchen and process garlic with oil, salt, pepper and sugar in a food processor or blender until smooth and light cream in colour. With motor running, add vinegar through the feed chute and, when combined, switch off and pour this rich dressing into a screw-top jar. Keeps, refrigerated, for about two weeks.

Nam jim dressing

3 cloves garlic, peeled and crushed

3 green chillies, seeded and roughly chopped

3 coriander roots, washed and trimmed

160 ml/5 fl oz freshly squeezed lime juice

60 ml/2 fl oz nam pla (fish sauce)

30 g/1 oz caster sugar

Makes about 250 ml/8 fl oz

Combine all ingredients and work to a rough paste. Serve immediately.

Orange and chive dressing

1 tsp mustard powder, dried

1 hard-boiled egg, roughly chopped

125 ml/4 fl oz freshly squeezed orange juice

1 tsp finely grated orange rind

250 ml/8 fl oz pouring cream

½ tsp salt

¼ tsp white pepper

2 Tbsp chopped chives

Makes about 440 ml/14 fl oz

Mash the mustard and egg together. Add orange juice and rind and mix well. Whisk in cream, salt, pepper and chives. Check and adjust the seasoning – you may like to add more orange juice. This dressing should be used immediately.

Blue cheese dressing

60 g/2 oz blue vein cheese, such as gorgonzola or Milawa blue

2 tsp white wine vinegar

250 ml/8 fl oz traditional vinaigrette (*see* page 287)

Makes about 310 ml/10 fl oz

Place cheese in a bowl and mash to a paste with the vinegar. When fully combined, stir in the vinaigrette. Pour into a storage container.

Shake the dressing well before using. It's the perfect dressing for a Cos lettuce and pear salad, among others. Keeps, refrigerated, for about two weeks.

Traditional vinaigrette

60 ml/2 fl oz olive oil,
  or vegetable oil

1 clove garlic, peeled and
  crushed

½ tsp dry Dijon mustard

1 Tbsp wine vinegar

1 Tbsp finely chopped parsley

½ tsp salt

¼ tsp white pepper

Makes about 80 ml/2½ fl oz

For the very best results, this dressing must be made by hand. Put the oil, garlic and mustard in a large bowl and whisk with a balloon whisk until the mixture is a creamy consistency and light yellow in colour. Whisking aerates and blends extremely well. Whisk in the vinegar and add parsley, salt and pepper. Stir until combined.

The best way to coat salad leaves with vinaigrette is to tumble them in a small amount of dressing. There should never be any dressing left sitting in the bottom of the bowl. Alternatively, serve the dressing separately and have guests help themselves. This way any leftover salad can be refrigerated and used at another meal.

Variations on the vinaigrette theme:
- Crumble two hard-boiled egg yolks into the dressing at the last minute. Dice the egg whites and add to the salad ingredients.
- Add 2 teaspoons each of finely chopped capers, gherkins and green olive flesh to the mixture at the last minute.
- Substitute 2 tablespoons of orange juice for the 1 tablespoon of vinegar if you like a citrus flavour.

Recipe accompaniments

Semi-roasted tomato salsa

140 g/5 oz semi-roasted
   tomatoes, roughly
   chopped

85 g/3 oz red onion,
   peeled and finely
   chopped

35 ml/¼ oz water
   chestnuts, drained and
   finely diced

1 Tbsp green chillies,
   minced

½ tsp paprika

½ Tbsp brown sugar

1 Tbsp brown vinegar

2 Tbsp vegetable oil

Makes 225–450 g/8–16 oz

Make this delicious salsa at least 4 hours before
you plan to use it. Just mix all the ingredients
together. The salsa will store in the refrigerator for
5 days.

Glass noodle salad

125 g/4 oz dried mung bean thread noodles

1 carrot, peeled and finely julienned

100 g/3½ oz daikon (Japanese white radish), peeled and finely julienned

½ cucumber, cut lengthwise, de-seeded and julienned

1 very small red onion, peeled and sliced very finely

40 g/1½ oz Japanese pickled ginger, julienned

70 g/2½ oz mangetout, washed and crisp from the refrigerator

1 red pepper, finely julienned

60 g/2 oz fresh coriander leaves

For the noodle salad dressing:

1 Tbsp palm sugar

120 ml/4 fl oz coconut cream

juice of 2 limes

1 Tbsp Nam Prik sauce

1–2 Tbsp fish sauce

Serves 4

Put the noodles into a large bowl and pour boiling water over to cover them. Set aside for 5–7 minutes and then strain noodles, running them under cold water to stop cooking. Ensure all the water is removed then transfer the noodles to a mixing bowl and allow to cool for 10 minutes.

Add all other ingredients except for the coriander leaves and dressing and toss gently using your hands.

Make the dressing by combining all the ingredients and mixing well. Pour over the assembled salad ingredients and toss gently, then top with the coriander leaves and serve.

Watermelon and feta salad

60 g/2 oz pumpkin seeds

sea salt and freshly ground black pepper

2 Cos lettuces (or 2 x 170g bags of Cos leaves), broken into leaves, washed and dried

½ small watermelon, rind removed and cut into small chunks

250 g/9 oz feta cheese (choose a firmish kind), patted dry and crumbled into chunks

3 Tbsp lemon-infused extra virgin olive oil (or use extra virgin olive oil with the zest of 1 lemon)

1 Tbsp white wine vinegar

short bamboo skewers, soaked in cold water for 30 minutes

Serves 6

Cook pumpkin seeds first in a lightly oiled saucepan over a medium heat until they cease popping, shaking pan occasionally (pan must be covered either with a splatter screen or lid, because seeds pop everywhere and they're hot!). Tip seeds onto a plate and sprinkle generously with sea salt.

Arrange cos leaves on a large platter. Lay watermelon slices on leaves, crumble feta over, then scatter over pumpkin seeds. Mix lemon-infused olive oil and white wine vinegar with ¼ teaspoon of sea salt and some black pepper. Pour this over the salad.

Spanish onion salad

250 g/8 oz dried green lentils, washed

625 ml/20 fl oz water

1 small red onion, roughly chopped

125 g/4 oz red pepper, diced

40 g/1½ oz mint leaves

125 ml/4 fl oz mayonnaise

60 ml/2 fl oz extra virgin olive oil

2 Tbsp Spanish sherry vinegar

1 tsp salt

½ tsp turmeric

Serves 4

For the salad, place lentils in a saucepan and add water. Bring to the boil and simmer for 20 to 25 minutes, skimming the top of the water during cooking to remove the brown froth. The lentils should be tender but holding their shape.

Remove from heat, strain and rinse under cold water for 30 seconds. Drain and pour into a salad bowl. Add onion and capsicum. Tear mint leaves into pieces as you add them to the lentils. Pour in the mayonnaise, oil, sherry vinegar, salt and turmeric. Stir well to combine flavours and set aside to cool to room temperature.

Rosemary aïoli

3 large organic egg yolks

1-2 cloves garlic, crushed

2 Tbsp lemon juice

75 ml/2½ fl oz extra virgin
    olive oil

125 ml/4 fl oz
    vegetable oil

2 Tbsp finely chopped
    fresh rosemary

¼ tsp salt

freshly ground black
    pepper, to taste

Makes 250 ml/8 fl oz

Whisk the egg yolks with the garlic and lemon juice until foamy. Slowly whisk in the oils in a thin stream, until mixture is thick and has emulsified. Whisk in rosemary, salt and pepper to taste. Cover and refrigerate until needed. Aïoli can be kept in the fridge for up to 2 days.

Nb. This recipe uses raw egg. To minimize the risk of salmonella, children, pregnant women, the elderly and the sick should avoid raw eggs. Make sure to use only farm-fresh, organic eggs.

Spicy black-eye bean paste

250 g/8 oz black-eye beans, soaked and strained

4 cloves garlic, poached

2 Tbsp lime juice

1 tsp cumin powder

1 tsp grated nutmeg

½ tsp ground white pepper

¼ tsp chilli powder

½ tsp salt

2 Tbsp extra virgin olive oil

1 Tbsp parsley, chopped

Makes 450–700 g/1–1½lb

Cook the beans covered in water at a simmer until they start to break down, about 40–60 minutes. Strain, and reserve a cup (250 ml/8 fl oz) of the cooking liquid.

Put all the ingredients except for the oil and parsley into a food processor and reduce to a paste. You may need to add some cooking liquid to make the paste the consistency you like; it should be smooth and creamy.

Remove the paste from the processor bowl into a serving bowl and smooth over the top. Spoon over the olive oil and sprinkle with the parsley. Serve with crusty bread or crackers.

Curried chickpeas

400 g/14 oz precooked chickpeas, drained

1 tsp coriander seeds, roasted

6 green cardamom pods, broken open

5 cm/2 in cinnamon stick, in pieces

7 whole cloves

1 tsp white peppercorns

1 tsp poppy seeds

5 cm/2 in fresh ginger, chopped

4 cloves garlic, chopped

1 small onion, chopped

2 Tbsp peanut oil or ghee

1 Tbsp black mustard seeds

salt (optional)

60g/2 oz whole mint leaves

Serves 4

Wash the chickpeas and set aside.

In a mortar and pestle, grind to a paste the coriander seeds, cardamom pods, cinnamon, cloves, white peppercorns, poppy seeds, ginger root, garlic and onion. Heat the oil in a saucepan to smoking point and add the black mustard seeds, then put the lid on the saucepan and cook for 30 seconds. Add the spice paste and chickpeas and cook for a further minute. Add enough water to completely cover the peas, reduce the heat and simmer with the lid on for 45 minutes. Check for seasoning and add salt if necessary.

You can serve this stunning curry on its own with the mint leaves tumbled over it, or with meats of your choice.

Spiced couscous

1 onion, peeled and
finely chopped

olive oil

1 clove garlic, peeled
and crushed

1 tsp each ground or
crushed coriander
seeds and fennel seeds

1/4 tsp chilli powder

salt

200 g/7 oz 'instant' (quick-
cooking) couscous

300 ml/10 fl oz stock,
heated (heat just before
using so it doesn't
evaporate)

1 Tbsp chopped mint,
plus extra for garnishing

1 Tbsp red wine vinegar

Serves 6

Put onion in a saucepan with 2 tablespoons of
olive oil and cover. Cook gently until it is
softened. Add garlic and crushed seeds, chilli
powder and 1/2 teaspoon salt. Continue cooking
gently for 10–15 minutes, until fragrant and pale
gold in colour. Add couscous, stir well, then tip in
hot stock. Bring to the boil, stirring, cover and turn
off heat. Leave to infuse for 15 minutes. Before
serving, stir through freshly chopped mint and
vinegar.

Caramelized onions

1 Tbsp butter

1 Tbsp olive oil

2 large onions, sliced into
1.5 cm/½ in rings

1 Tbsp balsamic vinegar

1 Tbsp brown sugar

Heat the butter and oil in a large frying pan over medium heat. Add the onions, stirring to coat. Sauté for 8–10 minutes, stirring occasionally, until softened and the edges begin to brown. Stir in the vinegar and sugar, cover and reduce the heat to low. Leave to cook slowly for 20–30 minutes, until the onions have collapsed and are meltingly tender.

Flatbread

2 tsp active dry yeast

100 ml/3½ fl oz warm
water

500 g/1 lb 2 oz plain flour

1½ tsp salt

1 Tbsp chopped
rosemary, thyme or
herb of choice

1 Tbsp extra virgin olive
oil, for oiling the bowl

200 ml/7 fl oz carbonated
water

Makes 4 flatbread

Sprinkle the yeast over the warm water and
leave for 5 minutes, or until foaming. Combine
the flour, salt and chopped herbs in a large bowl
and make a well in the centre. Stir the yeast
mixture and pour it into the well, with the olive oil
and 150 ml/5 fl oz carbonated water. Draw the
flour in from the sides, until it is all combined and
adding extra water if needed. Knead the dough
on a lightly floured surface for 10 minutes, or until
smooth and elastic. Put in a clean, oiled bowl
and leave to rise for about 1½ hours, or until
doubled in size. Punch the dough down and
leave for a further 10 minutes. Divide the dough
into four and, on a lightly floured surface, roll out
into rounds about 23 cm/9 in in diameter and
5 mm/¼ in thick. Cook for about 2–3 minutes on
the first side, using a fork to prick any bubbles
that form. Flip the bread over and cook for a
further 2 minutes.

Pizza base dough

2¼ tsp active dry yeast

275 ml/9 fl oz warm water

About 500 g/1 lb 2 oz
   plain flour

2 tsp salt

75 ml/2½ fl oz olive oil
   plus extra for oiling the
   bowl and brushing

Makes 6 x 20 cm/8 in pizza bases

Stir the yeast into the warm water, cover and let stand for 15 minutes until foaming. Combine the flour and salt in a large bowl. Slowly add the yeast mixture and olive oil alternately, stirring after each addition. Turn the dough out on to a lightly floured work surface and knead for 8 minutes, until the dough is soft and elastic. Place the dough in a big, lightly oiled bowl and leave to rise until doubled in size, about 1 hour.

Punch down the dough and divide into six balls. Flatten and shape them into circles, cover with clingfilm and leave to rest for 5 minutes. Shape the circles again so they are 20 cm/8 in in diameter. Brush with oil and grill for 2–3 minutes. Flip the dough over and add your pizza toppings on the cooked side. Brown the bottom of the dough.

Cinnamon courgette bread

375 g/12 oz small courgette, washed, trimmed and grated

3 eggs, beaten with 1 Tbsp olive oil

1 Tbsp sugar

1 tsp ground cinnamon

1 Tbsp finely grated Parmesan cheese

½ tsp salt

340 g/12 oz sifted self-raising flour

70 g/2½ oz walnuts, crumbled

olive oil spray

Makes 2 loaves

Preheat oven to 170° C

Mix together the courgette, eggs and oil, sugar, cinnamon, cheese and salt; stir to combine well. Mix in the flour and walnuts. Let mixture sit for 5 minutes.

Spray 2 bread tins (21 cm/8½ in long x 11 cm/4½ in wide and 10 cm/4 in deep) with olive oil. Spoon equal amounts of the courgette mixture into the tins and cook in the oven for 1 hour or until a skewer comes out clean.

Leave in tins for 10 minutes then turn out onto a cooking rack to cool before slicing. (Cinnamon courgette bread freezes very well.)

Index

Acknowledgments

Our thanks to:

Peter Howard - p.24-25, 26-27, 28-29, 30-31,
34-35, 36-37, 40-41, 48-49, 52-53, 54-55,
56-57, 64-65, 66-67, 68-69, 70-71, 72-73,
74-75, 76-77, 88-89, 92-93, 94-95, 102-103,
114-115, 120-121, 126-127, 128-129, 130-
131, 138-139, 140-141, 148-149, 150-151,
152-153, 154-155, 156-157, 158-159, 164-
165, 168-169, 170-171, 172-173, 178-179,
180-181, 184-185, 186-187, 200-201, 214-
215, 220-221, 226-227, 228-229, 230-231,
240-241, 242-243, 256-257, 260-261, 262-
263, 264-265, 272, 273, 280, 282, 283, 284,
285, 286-287.

Pippa Cuthbert and Lindsay Cameron-
Wilson - p. 32-33, 38-39, 44-45, 50-51,
58-59, 60-61, 78-79, 80-81, 82-83, 84-85,
86-87, 90-91, 96-97, 98-99, 100-101, 104-
105, 108-109, 110-111, 112-113, 116-117,
122-123, 160-161, 162-163, 166-167, 174-
175, 176-177, 182-183, 190-191, 192-193,
194-195, 196-197, 198-199, 202-203, 204-
205, 206-207, 218-219, 222-223, 224-225,
244-245, 254-255, 258-259, 266-267, 268-
269, 274, 275, 276, 277, 278, 279, 281.

Julie Biuso - p. 42-43, 46-47, 118-119, 132-
133, 134-135, 136-137, 208-209, 212-213,
216-217, 232-233, 234-235, 236-237, 238-
239, 250-251, 252-253.

Penny Oliver - p.106-107, 124-125, 142-143,
144-145, 246-247, 270-271.